A FAMILY LIKENESS

A FAMILY LIKENESS

A novel by
JANIS STOUT

**Texas
Monthly
Press**

Texas Monthly Press, Inc.
P.O. Box 1569
Austin, Texas 78767

A B C D E F G H

Stout, Janis P.
   A family likeness.

   I. Title.
PS3569. T659F3   813'.54   82-4888
ISBN 0-932012-26-4   AACR2

Book Design by Zilla Doonan and Mandy Wigginton

For Granny

Florence Druecilla Guthrie, born March 2, 1882, in Red River County, Texas. Married Virgil McCall, native of Tennessee, April 23, 1900. There are no records of what she looked liked then or how she felt about farming or marriage or any other matter, and there is no one who remembers. Mother of nine children. The first was born one Sunday morning early in December, 1901. An eighth-month baby, he died two days after birth, unnamed. Another male child, Lloyd Taylor McCall, died three days after birth in 1912; his twin, Floyd Tyler McCall, lived to be fifty-two years old, funloving and mean as hell. Five more, including Edna Earle. Widowed in 1920, when the oldest child was fourteen and the youngest just eighteen months. Married Jake Glover, possible native of a clearing in the piney woods near Deport, Texas, in 1923. Marriage annulled. The last child born in 1924, when she was forty-two years old. Sold the home place in 1932 and moved to Fort Worth to live in a rented house. Died February 16, 1959, ignorant and afraid of the hospital, a relic, incontinent, half-blind, half-deaf.

Part I

I

"**M**AMMA." EDNA EARLE WAITED, then stuck her head in through the open door. Over the sound of chicken frying and pots banging she shouted again, "Mam-ma! Isn't it time Elmo was home?"

"Oh, any time, honey. He'll be along."

She walked to the corner of the house and looked up the road the way he would come. No sign of him yet. She wished he would come on. Ora Lee strutted up the steps with the corn for supper, the last, tough ears off the burned-up stalks, and stuck out her tongue. "Miss Birthday Girl," she hissed. "Think you're so fine."

Edna Earle crimped her mouth and looked away. There was no use bothering with Ora Lee. She was just mad because she was having to do extra in the kitchen. Whoever's birthday it was didn't have to do anything. Which was the way it should be, of course.

If she couldn't get a rise out of Edna Earle, Ora Lee would try elsewhere. She turned on Cleora, who sat hemming with tiny stitches in the wide center hall. "Little twit thinks she's too good to work in the kitchen, too good to sweat."

Cleora never missed a stitch, but wagged a red pigtail back over her shoulder and trained her hard, blue twelve-year-old eyes on Ora Lee for half a minute, while her hands kept on sewing. "It ain't my fault I'm the only one can sew a decent hem," she said. Then she confided to her work, "Some people can't do nothin' right."

That was all the come-on Ora Lee needed. "One of these days I'm going to pull that red hair right outa your head, Cleora McCall. You just wait. I'm going to get you by them two pigtails and shake the pee outa you."

"Mamma," Cleora wailed, "Ora Lee's talking ugly to me."

Mamma called from the kitchen. "Come on with that corn, Ora Lee." She was used to it and didn't pay much mind.

Edna Earle smiled. She enjoyed thinking of Mamma in there cooking a special supper for her birthday and Ora Lee having to help while she stood on the porch and watched for the others. Fifteen years old today. August 5, 1931, and she was fifteen years old. She felt important and proud.

Leaning on the porch rail above the dry remains of the summer's flowers, she watched for Ruth and Jess, and for Elmo. From here, she would not be able to see him coming, because the road ran at an angle past the side of the house and he would be coming from the back. If she went around to the side, where Billie was dressing kittens in doll clothes on the unrailed stretch of the porch, she would be able to watch both ways. But she liked standing right here, by the steps. She felt like a queen. She would see Elmo when he rounded the corner of the house. Across the road, beyond the cross-fenced pasture and the main corn field, the cotton stood with glossy leaves under the late-day sun, the bolls swelling toward fall. Beyond that, just visible from the porch, stood the wall of thick pine woods. She would be able to see Ruth and Jess's wagon when it came through the dry crossing, just where the woods touched the road on both sides.

These days the road was deep in dust. Dust stood in the air and shimmered in the hot sun. It had been a terrible summer, dry and very hot. Everything planted was ruined and the earth itself was baking and cracking open. People were saying the summer of '31 would go down with the summer of '23. Some of them talked like it was the end of the world. Edna Earle did not believe that, but she knew it was bad. In the spring Mamma had filled their cleanly swept front yard with cannas, zinnias, petunias, four o'clocks—flowers all over, all mixed together. But by mid-July they had all drooped and shrivelled to dry stalks. No matter that she threw the dishwater out on them every evening, they could not be kept. Now there was only the twisted old crape myrtle, and it hardly bloomed at all any more.

Edna Earle stood above the withered flowers, looking intently down the road. Probably they would not bring her a present, she thought. How could they, with never a dime to their names, to hear them tell it. She hoped they would, but probably they wouldn't. Elmo might, though. He had been working at Badgett's store on Saturdays and two afternoons a week for two or three months now, ever since the doctor told old man Badgett to slow down. Badgett's was the only store in Cut Hand, and being right across the road from the grist mill (Badgett owned that, too) it did a good business. Elmo made three dollars a week keeping store while Mr. Badgett rested. Surely he would have kept some back to buy her a present! What was the use of being his favorite sister if he wouldn't do that?

Of course Mamma couldn't have bought her a present. Money from last year's cotton had run out back in the spring, the price had been down so, and they had been making it just on Elmo's storekeeping money and what Floyd brought in from pumping gas at Clamie two days a week. From time to time, both of the boys picked up a little extra money chopping wood for widow-women and old folks, but they were just barely getting by, and she knew Mamma could not spare a dime for a birthday present. There were things to be bought yet for Cleora and Billie, so they could start back to school. But maybe there would be something from Elmo.

She could smell the chicken frying. The aroma of it drifted clear out to the front porch through the long windows that stretched so low their sills were nearly on the floor. All the windows were open now in the hope of catching a breeze, though it didn't feel like there would ever be a breeze again. For the birthday dinner they were having chicken and greens and corn and sliced tomatoes and baking powder biscuits—a real spread. And Mamma had made her favorite dessert, blackberry cobbler. There wouldn't be a cake. The hens had not been laying good because of the heat, and they didn't have enough eggs to use up as many as it would take for a cake. If she looked in she could see Mamma moving past the kitchen door, fanning with her apron if her hands were empty. She could not see Ora Lee through the open front door, but could hear her resentfully banging plates onto the table. She wondered why Mamma had not called Billie to set the table. Billie wouldn't have minded; she would have made a game of it. But Mamma had left her playing with her kittens.

Finally, away down the road, lurching up from where the road dipped and the trees bent down close at the dry crossing, the wagon appeared, a puff of white dust keeping pace behind it. In a minute Edna Earle could make out Jess and Ruth on the seat. Virgie would be in Ruth's lap, lulled to sleep by the swaying of the wagon. As she stuck her head in the door and called, "They're coming, Mamma," Billie let the kittens go and ran down the front steps and out to the gate so she could be the first to see the baby.

At the same time, Elmo rounded the corner of the house and rode across to the barn. He looked up at Edna Earle as he went by, but gave her no sign, not even a birthday grin. He would take care of the horse, wash up on the stoop, and then come in through the back door.

Mamma emerged, wiping her hands on her apron. "I thought you

said they was here," she grumbled. "I coulda finished making out the
biscuits. Cleora, you put away that sewing now and come out here
and say hello to your sister." She passed her arm across her forehead
and shaded her eyes with her long and bony right hand, standing easi-
ly with her pot-shaped paunch thrust forward and her left fist on her
hip.

They drew up in front of the gate, and Jess hitched the team while
Ruth got herself and the baby down from the wagon. Jess carried up a
Woolworth sack and a jar of Ruth's watermelon rind preserves, which
he handed to Cleora as he came up the steps. Then he touched his hat
to Mrs. McCall, directed a terse happy birthday at Edna Earle and sat
down in one of the porch rockers, where he commenced staring grimly
down the dirt road he had just driven. Ruth came beaming up with the
baby, a lumpy bundle wrapped in a quilt despite the heavy August
heat. She surrendered him to his grandmother, who poured out a
greeting in baby talk, kissed him hard on the forehead, and handed
him down to Edna Earle before getting back to the kitchen.

Edna Earle wasn't sure what to do with the baby. He had started to
squirm at Mamma's hard kiss and was now working up a cry, and she
was stuck with him. Ruth had disappeared into the kitchen with
Mamma. They always got off to themselves, like two best friends who
shared a great secret, or like members of a club with its own code
words. They would whisper together, sometimes pursing their lips
and shaking their head identically, as if disgusted. It left Edna Earle
feeling like an outsider. Now Jess had taken the best rocker and was
just about asleep in it, and the baby was tuning up good and proper.
She liked holding him when he was full and content, lying against her
like one of her old rag dolls, but when he cried she wanted nothing to
do with him. She took the other rocker and tried to soothe him back
to sleep while Cleora and Billie hovered around, hoping she would
give up and let one of them have a go at it. When rocking wouldn't do,
she tried stretching him on his stomach across her knees, the way she
had seen Mamma do it, but he stiffened and screamed.

"You're going to drop him if you don't watch it," Cleora told her.
"You'd better let me have him."

"What do you think you could do that I can't, smartie?" She would
have been glad to get rid of the baby, but not if it meant giving Cleora
a chance to show off. She resumed rocking, patting his back harder,
hoping to make him burp. Cleora, in a pout, went back into the hall to

her sewing.

Elmo had come out to the porch and was leaning against the post at the corner. From time to time he looked over his shoulder at her. His attentions made her feel self-conscious and proud; she began to talk to the squalling bundle like Mamma always did. "Pitty ittle man, what does oo want?" She pretended to be fully occupied with the baby and not to notice Elmo, who had walked around behind her and was dangling a finger into the little fist.

Billie wandered off, leaving the porch to the two of them and the snoring Jess. They could hear her around the corner, trying to roust her kittens out from under the house, where they had taken refuge.

Elmo stood behind her chair and pulled the special twig of hair that he always pulled to tease her, but not very hard, like he was thinking about something else. Then he ambled back to the post and looked down the road. "Wonder what's keeping Floyd," he said.

Finally Ruth came out and scooped up the baby and said, with a giggle, that she would go give him some titty. "You know what?" she added. "I brung you a birthday present." She disappeared into the house again, and Edna Earle heard a door close somewhere inside: they had not been brought up to display such things. Jess snorted, shook his head, and went back to sleep.

"Wonder what's keeping Floyd," Elmo said again. He was trying to get Edna Earle's attention, wanting her to talk to him. But she was preoccupied with the surprising news that Ruth had brought her a present. How did she know what was keeping Floyd? What difference did it make? Elmo waited a while, slumped against the post, then, without turning, said, "Hey."

No answer.

"Hey, Edna Earle, listen. I want to talk to you about something. Come over here, why don't you." He led her around to the side porch, and they sat on the edge, dangling their feet. Elmo wanted to tell her a big secret, but he couldn't think how to start. He had decided something big and important, and he had to tell Edna Earle first. He always told her first, whatever it was.

She sat swinging her feet and admiring her black patent dress-up shoes and wondering what Ruth could have brought her. She liked being the center of attention in her blue dotted-swiss dress and last spring's patent leather shoes, even if they did pinch her toes.

"Listen, I want to tell you something," he started. But she didn't pay

attention, she was too tied up in the question of Ruth's present. He
tried again. "You know what I'm thinking about?"

"Oh, let me guess. Let's see."

He tried to grin and wait, but it was hard to be patient. She was
making a joke out of this, and he wasn't joking.

"I know. You were thinking about the pet gosling, the one that ran
after us when we played around-the-house, and we caught up with it
and someone jumped off the porch right here and landed on it and
squashed it."

"No, that wasn't it. I—"

"What do you think it is?"

"What?"

"What Ruth brought me, of course! I can't think what."

He felt like slamming his fist against the floor and going off by
himself. But instead he dangled some bait to catch her attention. He
had brought her a present, too, he said. She took the bait, but then
would not let go of it to talk about anything else. What was it? Where
was it? When did he buy it? So it was no real interruption when Ora
Lee came out yelling for them to come in to supper.

"Yoo-hoo," Mamma warbled from inside. "Come on to supper
while it's hot. Where on earth could that Floyd be?"

"Here he comes now, Mamma," Edna Earle called back. He was just
tying his horse at the gate.

To Elmo's question of what had kept him, Floyd only frowned and
said they'd talk about it after supper. Then he turned on Edna Earle
with a show of high spirits. "How's that little bit o' nothin' on her
birthday? Had a birthday lickin' yet? I'm just the one to do it." He
made to grab her, but she ran in, giggling like wild.

She loved for Floyd to tease her, if he didn't keep it up too long and
get rough. It was exciting to have a brother nineteen years old, grown
up and his own man and wild. Elmo used to play with her like that,
too; they used to tussle and roll over and over together, coming up
flushed and out of breath. But Elmo had gotten so quiet and mopey
that he wasn't fun anymore. Ora Lee called him Old Sobersides. And
what good was a brother like that? Floyd and Elmo looked so much
alike—short, scarcely over five feet, wiry, with thin lips and hard,
close-set eyes (Floyd's glittery with meanness). It was hard to believe,
sometimes, that they could be so different.

They all went in to supper, with Jess bringing up the rear, yawning and stretching. It was a good meal, everybody's favorites, but even better than usual because it had been made special for her birthday. The cobbler was from blackberries they had picked in the spring, that Mamma had put up in jars. They were still almost as good as when they were picked. Besides the blackberry cobbler Mamma had surprised them by making tea cakes, big flat sugar cookies that everybody loved. She had done the extra baking that morning while they were out working in the garden.

Last of all, as they passed around the tea cakes, Ruth said, "Now let me get out what I brung you." She brought the Woolworth sack from under the bed in the front room and laid it on the table in front of Edna Earle. There was a hush of anticipation.

What she pulled out was a pile of rags. No, not just rags, she realized, but pieces all cut to size and shape, and a few sewn together to form a flower. Ruth beamed. "Your first quilt! I cut out the whole top for you and pieced that one square and pinned all the rest together in bunches for the squares."

Edna Earle just managed to thank her and say she was real proud to have it. She ruffled through the little cut out pieces, trying to look interested.

She hated quilts! What she wanted was a purplish satin downcomforter like the one she had seen in the store window in Clarksville. What fun would there be in making a tacky old quilt? Now Cleora, that would have been just the thing for her. Cleora would sit for hours taking the tiniest stitches ever, tinier even than Ruth's, with her mouth drawn up like a fancywork French knot.

"Well," she said again, "I do thank you, Ruth." She hoped it sounded better than she felt.

While Elmo went out to get the present he had brought, Mamma lamented having nothing to give. "Not ary a thing, honey, and I hate it so bad." In later years Edna Earle would say they had been so poor they never got anything for birthdays, but that was not true; most years they did. It was the lack of what she was used to being able to provide that made Mamma feel so bad.

Elmo's package was flat and just the right size for what she hoped it was. She looked up to see if everybody was watching. Now that the excitement of the quilt was over, Ruth was starting to do the dishes, but the other girls craned their necks to see. Yes, it was just what she had hoped: three thick tablets of paper and a box of pencils. "School supplies!" she crowed. Elmo turned and went out to the porch. Knowing she was pleased was enough; he was too self-conscious to stay for more.

Ora Lee said in dismay that she had thought it would be hairpins or a dress length, something like that. But school supplies! Just count on Elmo to do some crazy thing!

"Don't you say that, Ora Lee!" She stood up, clutching the tablets against her. "Don't you talk Elmo down! He knew what I wanted; nobody else did."

Mamma shushed her. "Listen, honey," she said soothingly. "Set down here a minute. We might as well have this out right now. We've been over it and over it, and there's not any way you can get to school this year. There's just not any way, and you might as well face it."

Ruth reached over her shoulder, clearing the dishes away. "You already finished all the grades anyway," she said, pausing in mid-reach before she picked up the last stack, as if that statement put an end to the discussion.

"Amen," said Ora Lee. "I'm thankful I'm done."

Billie continued uncertainly, "I don't know. History's nice, all those battles and explorers. And recess."

Edna Earle scowled and shrugged her off. Billie didn't understand a thing.

Cleora sucked in her breath with a tiny whistle, signalling that she was about to pronounce the right and wrong of the matter. "We're supposed to go to school when we're little," she stated, "but when we're done we oughta stay here and help Mamma. I know I will."

Then Jess cleared his throat and sat up importantly, because he was the oldest male present and therefore the giver of the final word. "Now, Edna Earle, you may think it's not my place to tell you what to do," he began, "but since there ain't no man of the house around here—"

"There is, too," she said. "There's Elmo."

"Well, I like that!" Floyd complained. After all, he was older. But no one paid him any mind. Mamma said shush and listen to their brother-in-law.

He huffed and sat solemnly for a minute. "Well, you know I prize learnin' as much as any." He had been innocent of reading and writing when he married Ruth; she had taught him at night by a kerosene lamp on the kitchen table. "But you done the seventh over twice, didn't you? You finished our school. Seems like that's enough. That's all Miss Trueman can do for you, she said so herself."

Edna Earle knew what he meant. Miss Trueman had given her a copy of *Elsie Dinsmore* and had written in it, "For Edna Earle McCall, for completing the Course of Study at the Public School of Cut Hand, Texas, June 5, 1931."

"Yes, but—"

"Yes, I know, Edna Earle," Mamma interrupted. She had listened to Jess long enough. "You want to go to high school at Clamie. But we done been all through that, and you know it. How do you think you could get to Clamie ever day of the week?"

She had been planning for a long time what she would say if the chance ever came. She had figured it out that a high school diploma was her ticket away from here to the places of satin down-comforters and ready-made clothes, a store-window world that she would step into so people on the outside would admire and envy her. Now it was time to fight for what she had to have. "I could go with Jess on his milk run three days a week."

At that, Jess looked more awake than he had all day. "Well, now, I don't know about that," he said. Ruth stacked dishes with a great significant clatter.

Elmo had come in from the porch and stood ready to support her in whatever she wanted. "Why couldn't she go with Jess?" he demanded.

Jess then discovered that everybody was looking at him. "Well, now, it's about a—" he pulled out the watch that Ruth had bought him with her egg money when he learned to read, "about a good hour drive to Clamie, maybe two by the time I stop for milk along the way." He tucked the watch back into its little pocket. "Yessir, near two hour. Then a hour back in the evenin'. That's too much, don't you reckon?"

Ruth turned toward them with dripping hands. "And what about when the water gets up in the creek? You can't expect Jess to come through that back road in any kind of weather."

"I already figured that out, too," Edna Earle said. "I'll walk up and meet him on the main road. I won't care about the weather."

"Well, I swan," said Mamma. "You got a answer for everthing."

"Jess," Edna Earle begged, "you will think about it, won't you? I won't be no trouble. I can't do seventh again, Miss Trueman said she couldn't help me with algebra or diagramming or nothing anymore, and I just can't quit. I got to go to school if . . ." If what, she didn't really know. But she had seen Miss Trueman's pointed shoes and her soft hands, and she knew that Miss Trueman had been to high school. "Will you just think about it?" Her lips trembled, and her black eyes misted over. She sniffed deeply.

Mamma could never stand tears. "I don't know about all this high school business, missy," she told her, "but Jess'll think it over. Maybe we can work it out. I don't know how I'd get you any clothes to start in. I don't know how I'm a-goin' to get Cleora and Billie any either, for that matter, and they have to go. But we'll see, we'll see."

Everybody let out a breath all at once and knew it was settled that she could go. Ruth sniffed, put upon. She said it was time they were getting back, it was getting on toward dark.

While Ruth wrapped up the baby, Billie ran out to pet the horses one last time. Cleora went to throw the scraps to the chickens, and Ora Lee started dragging the tubs in for baths. She was in a hurry to get cleaned up and dressed before any of Floyd's friends came by. Edna Earle sat alone at the table absently eating her fourth tea cake. It had been a nice birthday supper, and the part about school had gotten over with easier than she expected.

Then she overheard Floyd saying low, while he followed Jess out to the wagon, "Heard today that Jake Glover was seen over in Clarksville this week. I ain't told Mamma yet." She could tell by the way Jess held his head that he was listening close, and she couldn't remember Floyd's face ever looking so serious. She hadn't heard the name in so long that she had to repeat it to herself—Jake Glover? Jake Glover?—before she called to mind who it was they were talking about. They were talking too low to hear now, their heads together confidentially, and when they stopped and spoke to Elmo, he too looked up quickly and walked on out with them.

It bothered her that Floyd had waited till he had Jess off alone to tell him about it. Why wouldn't he just say right out whatever it was? But she didn't think about it for long. It was more interesting to think about being fifteen years old and almost a woman, and about getting to go to the high school next month, maybe. Ruth pecked her on the cheek on her way out, just a peck because she was still put out about her riding to school with Jess; it was not even possible for her to conceive that Edna Earle did not absolutely adore the quilt pieces. When she and Jess drove off they all went in and finished up the dishes while

Floyd and Elmo toted in the bathwater.

Ora Lee set up the washtubs in the bedroom and gathered washrags and gray homemade soap, while Mamma heated the water a little by pouring in a kettleful from the stove. Billie and Cleora went first, sitting with averted faces while Mamma sudsed Billie and Cleora scrubbed herself red. As an end to the ritual, Mamma held up a towel while Billie stepped out into a flour-sacking nightgown. Cleora screened her own clean nakedness so scrupulously that even Ora Lee, straining covertly to see whether any fuzz had appeared around her crotch, could see nothing between knees and armpits. Lastly, Ora Lee and Edna Earle undressed quickly, screening themselves even more carefully because they had more to screen, and dipped in and out of the same water and into clean drawers and worn print dresses that they would wear again on Sunday afternoon and then to work in on Monday.

As she washed and dressed and combed through her wet hair, Edna Earle could hear Floyd out on the porch talking fast but low, and laughing, and Elmo pacing restlessly along the three turns of the porch, probably not so much listening to Floyd as tolerating his presence. Then Mamma told them to come empty the tubs, and they drew fresh water and bathed quickly while the girls went out to sit on the porch. When the boys finished they emptied and filled one last tub of water; then Mamma stopped shelling peas and had her bath. Her hair was still very damp, almost wet, when she reappeared in her clean, faded dress. It was the one time every week when any of them saw her hair released from its knot in back and hanging fuzzy over and past her shoulders.

Edna Earle liked to watch her mother while she combed out her hair, collecting balls of it in her lap that she would throw under the house later. She wasn't a handsome woman, not like the women pictured in the Sears and Roebuck catalog. She had light gray eyes, hair that was graying fast, and a long, humped nose. Her hands were hard and her arms, when she wore short sleeves, looked ropy with strength. It was good to look at her, so strong and with her hair let down. Edna Earle felt stirred, thinking how Mamma could run a farm and keep them all together and all in line, and still only a woman. She herself would never be tall and strong like that, she guessed. She had stopped growing years ago, but she wasn't near as tall as Ora Lee, even, and Ora Lee wasn't as tall as Mamma. But it didn't matter. She would live in town, Clarksville or maybe even Paris, and have store-bought clothes and town furniture. She wouldn't need to be big and strong and do a man's work.

Floyd came around the corner of the house from out back and stepped up onto the side porch. He pulled a chinaberry switch and went over to lean against the porch rail beside Elmo, switching the toes of his shoes. It was just good dark. Ora Lee sat on the top step, glancing toward the road every so often. She had tied back her hair with a red ribbon. A car went by, plowing deep in the sandy ruts and careening slightly, going too fast for the road.

"That was Billy Jack Epps, I bet," Ora Lee said softly. "He goes to see Janey Byers sometimes." Nobody responded; Floyd, who also went to see Janey sometimes, switched the toe of his shoe. Ora Lee sighed. "We don't ever have no company."

"Well, lookin' down the road won't make 'em come," Floyd told her. "You ready to go, Elmo?" Their horses were standing saddled by the front gate.

Elmo looked over at Mamma, combing her hair in the good rocker, and at Edna Earle. "I reckon so," he said.

Mamma cleared her throat and said sharply, without looking at him, "Now, Floyd, ain't no use in you goin' off with that bunch and gamble away your wood-choppin' money like you done last Saturday."

"Aw, Mamma."

"Ain't no use in it. All you'll do is go stand around in front of Badgett's store and talk nastiness and gamble away your money."

He didn't answer, just went on out where the horses were tied, with Elmo following. "She thinks that's all we'll do, huh?" he said to Elmo, and they rode out.

Mamma snorted pettishly and told Ora Lee to go light a lamp. "No use settin' here in the dark."

Cleora asked if they could light two so she could take one in and read a chapter before bed. She always read the Bible on Saturday night. It was the only book in the house except for Mamma's *Saint Elmo* and Edna Earle's *Elsie Dinsmore*. There were a few illustrated sheets under the boys' mattress, but no one else knew about those.

"Take Billie in with you, she's sleepy."

Then Elmo rode back across by the gate and toward the barn. "It's me, Mamma," he called as he passed.

"Hmmp," she grunted, though Edna Earle could see that she was pleased he had come back. But she never showed it, at times like that, not to any of them, and Elmo was always having to work for the favor he deserved better than all the rest, while Floyd got more than he deserved or even wanted. And Billie was loved best of the girls because she was the baby. Edna Earle noticed; she could see it. She should have been the favorite, she thought. Not Cleora, of course, even if she would have been the youngest without Billie. She was sure that she would have been the favorite if Mamma hadn't married that old Jake Glover. Then she would be getting that special love that Billie was getting. Papa would have wanted her to. But Virgil McCall had died when she was only three. First he had had measles, then he had tried to get back to work too soon—work always pressing on him from every side—and had gone out to the fields during a spell of damp spring weather and caught pneumonia. She couldn't even remember him. And Mamma had married Jake Glover. She sniffed, thinking of it, digging at that inner trench of resentment against Billie that would never be filled in.

In a few minutes Elmo came back to the house. "Been a big day, ha'n't it, Little Sister? I bet you're about ready for bedtime." Hinting for her to go on in, she knew.

"Oh, not yet."

He walked across the front stretch of the porch a couple of times, stood loitering behind her chair, wound around his finger a twig of her black hair that she had been braiding and unbraiding. Finally he spoke what was on his mind. "Mamma, did Floyd tell you who Alvin saw in town the other day?"

Ora Lee perked up. "Who?" she asked.

Mamma gave no sign of curiosity about who had been seen, but by sure instinct knew that she wanted to send the girls away before she found out. "You two girls get on to bed," she said. "It's been a big day."

"I don't want to, not yet. After all, it's my birthday."

"Well," Ora Lee flung at her, "what difference does that make?"

"Go on now, both of you."

Mamma's word was final then, but Ora Lee announced that she had to go out back first. She flounced over to the edge of the porch and jumped off.

Elmo followed Edna Earle in as far as the bedroom door. "Wait," he said, in a low whisper. He looked at the floor for a minute. She knew he was preparing to tell her something important, shaping the words before he began, and she felt impatient, as they all did with his carefully planned and self-conscious speech. At the same time she felt proud, knowing that his groping after the right words was a silent and thinking pause rather than the empty hawking and spitting of the neighbor men and boys. "Edna Earle," he started at last, "I've done made up my mind now. I'm goin' to talk to Brother Young the first chance I get about takin' up the sacred calling. It says in the Book, 'Go therefore,' and I'm goin' and can't Floyd nor nobody else talk me out of it." He paused and drew a long breath.

She felt she ought to say something. He was waiting. At last she said, all too lamely, "Well, I can imagine you a preacher, all right. I sure can. You a preacher and me a schoolteacher and livin' in town. We'll really be comin' up in the world, won't we?"

He flung his hand impatiently. That wasn't what he wanted at all. "You're the first one I've told," he said. "Not even Mamma yet."

Ora Lee came in suddenly from the back and demanded crossly what were they standing around in there for. "Always getting off somewhere, just the two of you. Go on, I want to go to bed."

Elmo stormed off. Nobody could ever talk to anybody around there! He banged the screen door behind him so hard it bounced. Ora Lee laughed. But Edna Earle, taking his part as usual, told her she didn't have to be so cranky. "What got your nose out of joint, anyway?"

"It ain't. I just had to do my share and yours, too, today, Miss Priss the Birthday Girl, and now I'm tired. So you let me alone, you hear?"

For a long time Edna Earle lay in bed listening to Mamma and Elmo talking on the front porch, a droning that drifted in through the long open window from the other end of the porch. They kept their voices low, and she caught only a few words now and then. She resisted sleep, prolonging the day, but it was hard not to drift off.

So she was the only one Elmo had told about his great ambition. She squirmed a little, pleased at being so much the favorite sister. Of course, she had always known she was. She remembered how, last spring, when they were picking blackberries on the way back from the cotton field, she got her dress caught in the brambles and he came to get it loose and stood feeding her blackberries from his pail. He poked the berries into her mouth, and she sucked the juice off the tips of his fingers as he drew them out again. "Open, little bird," he had said, and pushed the ripe blackberries into her mouth. They felt breathless, and they laughed, eating blackberries under the hot sun. She remembered, too, how she had waked up in the middle of the night, more than once, to see him standing at the door of the bedroom, watching her in her sleep. She knew he wasn't watching Ora Lee, just her. He was a good brother. He took care of her.

Now Ora Lee had gone right to sleep beside her. No matter how mad she got at somebody or, at other times, how much tickling and giggling she did when they were getting ready for bed, she always fell sound asleep right off.

It had been a good birthday even if she didn't get many presents. Her favorite supper and tea cakes besides the cobbler. In the morning she and the other girls had worked in the garden, weeding, picking beans and tomatoes for Mamma to put up for winter. This afternoon she had sat in the kitchen watching Mamma cut rolled-out pie dough in strips and lay them on top of the blackberries and juice. The half a dozen flies that buzzed over the partly assembled cobbler dispersed when Mamma waved her towel but came right back. She liked to watch Mamma work in the kitchen, moving surely, patting out the dough with neither haste nor hesitation. Sometimes they talked then, while she worked, and it was especially nice to sit in the kitchen and talk if Mamma was making something special.

Mamma and Elmo murmured on the porch, their voices blending with the monotonous and soothing drone of night things. She felt herself nearly asleep and wished drowsily that, now fifteen, she could feel like a different person going to sleep from that fourteen-year-old who lay here last night.

Once she stirred a little from sleep to listen again to their talk. Elmo was walking up and down the porch again. "What do you reckon he's comin' around for?" he asked, close to the window. Mamma said something. Who were they talking about? She turned over and almost settled again for sleep. Oh, yes, it must be Jake Glover. Floyd had been telling Jess something about that before, she remembered now.

Mamma raised her voice. "I'm tellin' you, I had enough trouble from that man. Now you just let him alone till he goes off again, you hear?"

Elmo kept walking up and down; Edna Earle could hear his steps and something being said that she couldn't make out. Hoots of owls down in the pine woods drifted in through the long window. She was nearly asleep again when his footsteps came up close to the window and stopped. "Well, I'll just say this much. If he lays a hand on Edna Earle—or any of you—I'll kill him."

"Don't you talk like that, Elmo Earl McCall. Don't you ever. The Lord hears them words, ever one of 'em."

Then they were quiet for a long time. Edna Earle, too sleepy to dwell on the menace in their talk, went off to sleep. It was just the two of them then, sharing the darkness, waiting for Floyd to come in. Mamma sat straight in the rocker, not bothering to rock, too tired to stay up any longer but too gratified by the sensation of rest to lose it in sleep.

Elmo stood with one foot propped on the porch rail and his chin in his hand. "Mamma," he said, "I'm goin' to talk to Brother Young about takin' up the calling."

She sat savoring it for a while, without answering, then stood up and patted him once on the shoulder before going in. "I'm real proud, Elmo," she said.

II

JAKE GLOVER WAS BILLIE'S FATHER. Edna Earle could not remember him clearly; he had been there so briefly. She was barely seven years old when Mamma married him. Ten months later Billie was born. But by then Glover was already back in Terrell State Hospital.

They never knew much about him, and sometimes, after she got old enough to think about such things, Edna Earle wondered why her mother had married a stranger like that. Not that she thought of it often. When she overheard Floyd telling Jess in a low voice that he had heard Glover was back, it was like coming across an old newspaper clipping forgotten between the pages of a dusty book.

He had shown up at church one Sunday in midsummer, looking worn and generally down on his luck. He was a thin, stooped man whose arms swung palms-back instead of palms-in when he walked. He told everyone who would listen that he had folks south of Talco but the farm wasn't doing any good and so he took off to find work. He spoke quietly, cutting his eyes from one to another of the congregation to see how they were reacting to him. Then after service, old man Byers, who had driven up too late to hear the story before time to go in, said his wife's people knew some Glovers at Paris that had relatives somewhere down around Talco and he thought they spoke well enough of them, of the Paris Glovers that is. So Hubert Ott said he guessed Miz McCall could use a hand getting a few things fixed up around her place but he didn't reckon she could pay much of anything.

Glover had come up quiet to where Mrs. McCall was just handing Cleora up to sit by Ruth on the seat of the wagon to drive home and get dinner. He asked if he could have just meals and a quilt to sleep on in the barn, for only a day or two if she didn't think he was worth that much any longer or if she couldn't afford help any longer, because he needed a meal and a place to stay bad and he was a good hand. Three months later they were married, and three months after that, after she had begun to feel uneasy about the way he acted at times, she found out that he had escaped from the state hospital for crazy people at Terrell and already had two wives and quite a number of children.

She had looked him over that first day, that day he came up to her at church, and had thought, well, he don't want much, might as well get some things done around the place. And when he had been there awhile, with his unshaven weasel face and too-big overalls, she had looked at him and shuddered; but then she looked again and thought about his fence mending and his weed chopping and his wood splitting. She considered. She weighed one thing against another. If he stayed on, if she married him, would he expect it to be the regular way of husbands and wives? She supposed he would. She would just have to put up with it.

And he was glad to stay. But he acted so strange sometimes, and he got stranger. She had to keep her eye on him, to see he didn't whip the children or take to petting on the girls. He knew she was watching him. He would turn his head and catch her with her eye on him, and grin meanlike, slylike. And in the nights he snorted and squealed, he wouldn't keep quiet, he didn't care that the children might hear.

Still she waited. Not long now till plowing. Better this than no man at all. But when she saw him one day with his fly open, showing himself to Ora Lee, she couldn't wait anymore. She got word to Hubert Ott and sent Ruth off with him one four a.m. to get the sheriff, to send Glover back to Terrell.

He must have heard Ott's wagon stop to pick up Ruth. He ran to the door with a shotgun, raving that it was robbers—"When we never had nothin' no robbers would have wanted, no more'n we do now," Floyd said—and fired once after them. Then he lighted a lamp and made them all get up and stand in a row, all but Ora Lee silently rolling their eyes at Mamma to see by her face just how scared they ought to be, but Ora Lee bawling steadily, while he held the lamp up to the face of each one and counted aloud, getting their names all wrong, and counted again every time it only came out five. "Weren't it six, Maw?" he would say, and count them over while Mamma followed him up and down the row, with the one thick braid she let down at night hanging over her left shoulder, and tugged at him to come back to bed. But he wouldn't, and if one of them, sleepy, dropped out of line, he delivered a smart slap on the cheek and began again with the lamp and the counting to five and the mixed-up names, the shotgun still under his left arm and loaded. Then just before daylight he said, "Yessir, I know they was six of 'em and they's a gal gone. White slavers, it was." Then Mamma whispered to him and tugged at his arm, flapping her hand at Floyd behind her back, and Glover turned toward her while Floyd herded them all outside. Big-eyed, they saw Mamma gazing hard after them in her coarse faded only nightgown, with the glow of the kerosene lamp falling on her neck and shoulder, where Jake Glover fumbled under the single thick braid.

He was still asleep in bed when the sheriff took him by the wrist. Mamma was in the kitchen making biscuits.

So Billie was born seven months after that, and then it was all the same as before except that now the gaunt woman, once redheaded but graying fast, had seven besides herself to provide for from the proceeds of the annual cotton crop that she made singlehanded.

All through August, after they heard Glover was around, they went through the work of every day watchful and uneasy, while the cotton bolls swelled. Elmo and Floyd, at the jobs that were barely keeping the family going until the cotton money came in, listened for news of him. From time to time they would bring home reports that he had been seen in Clamie or in Clarksville or beside a road. Mamma went about her picking and canning distractedly, with lips drawn into a tight purse, and the girls, watching her, wondered what it was that they were all afraid would happen if he came.

Ora Lee was the worst. Maybe she could remember better than the others that night when they went off for the sheriff. Assigned to keep birds away from the fruit that was spread to dry in pans set on one side of the porch and along the edge of the roof, she spooked at the sound of someone whistling on the road and ran to hide in the back stall in the barn, leaving the fruit for their winter pies to be pecked and fouled.

Through the last two weeks in August, in a spell of debilitating cloudy heat, until all the remaining beans and peas and tomato vines burned and withered in the garden patch, Mamma sweated over steaming kettles of mason jars, canning the vegetables she hoped would last them through the winter. Even Billie dragged while doing the outdoor work that was increased for everybody by the boys going off to jobs. Only Cleora sat on the porch, her slick red head bent over the buttonholes and hems she meticulously stitched in the garments Mamma had made in odd work-free moments. Ora Lee, passing the corner of the porch where Cleora sat, would stick out her tongue and hiss names at her: "Little twit, you wouldn't trouble yourself enough to go pee." But Cleora would only say that really she would rather be digging potatoes but she was the only one that could keep watch for Jake Glover because she wasn't scared of him like some people.

Then it was time for school to start. For Cleora and Billie that meant going off in flour-sack dresses—the first time ever that had happened. For Edna Earle it meant going to high school in Clamie in an old dress of Ora Lee's, hemmed up, and last spring's too-tight patent leather shoes. She cheered herself with thinking that there would be money for new clothes when the cotton was in and sold. But when she asked if she could have a new coat out of the cotton money, Mamma stopped peeling potatoes and looked at her hard for about two minutes. "You listen here," she said. "You wanted to go over to that school, and we're doing the best as ever we can to get you there. But Cleora and Billie has to have shoes, and there's not going to be money for extras—prob'ly not enough for all you rightly need—not and hang on to anything to see us through the winter. I don't know how we're a-goin' to get by, I don't for a fact. Things ain't like they used to be."

It was a momentous and complicated time for Edna Earle. Every day that she went to the new school she had to face the question of whether she should have gone. She had no friends, and it appeared she would never get a hold on geometry. More important was the great change in herself. A late developer, she had finally begun to menstruate.

Mamma had left her in ignorance, as she had all the girls, in the belief that some things are better left unsaid, or if possible un-acknowledged. So when Edna Earle felt the warm wet spot spreading in her drawers and, looking in, saw blood, she ran crying to Mamma. Something was wrong, she had hurt herself! Mamma cried, and said she just couldn't stand to tell her about the monthly sickness before. Then she explained that the blood, together with the pain of childbirth and the necessity of "having to do with men," were her punishment for Eve's sin in the Garden. Edna Earle's mind whirled at the un-fairness of suffering from something that had happened so long ago.

In the early fall, they dragged the long cotton sacks across the field for nearly two weeks, with Mamma picking a man's load besides cooking, washing, and caring for the stock and the chickens. The Cut Hand school met only for half days then, so the pupils could go home and help get the cotton in. Of course, some were kept home altogether

to help pick. Not Cleora and Billie. They were out at the main road
every morning at seven. But when the bus put them down again
before noon, they were into their oldest clothes and out to the field,
stopping only long enough to grab a snack on the way.

When Edna Earle came home from school late in the evenings, after
Jess dropped her off at the side of the house on his way home, Elmo
would always ask if she'd had a nice day, if everything was all right,
and whether she needed him to do her chores so she could work on her
studies. Sometimes she said yes, and opened a book and filled a few
lines on her tablet paper with pencilling and erasures.

But on the days she didn't go to school, it was out to the field to get
the cotton in. There had been some cool mornings, but now it turned
hot again, and the dust churned up and settled on her, while the
sweat ran down her face and arms in little muddy streams. She picked
until when she straightened up she cried, and her straight black hair
was snowy with puffs of white in spite of the bonnet. It fired her with
an implacable hatred of poor-white field work. Town women did not
work, they stayed in their houses and did the things that women are
supposed to do. It pained her to think of being seen working in the
field; she held herself bent and low, and refused to turn and wave
when wagons passed on the road. Miss Trueman did not work in the
fields. She had been to high school, and now she wore pointed shoes
and shirtwaists, and handed out books and wrote on the board.

From two rows away Mamma hollered and flung off her cotton
sack. It jerked them all up together from the trance in which they had
been working, and they stood stunned in their places, shading their
eyes. She was all in gyrations and shrieks, batting at her sides and
arms, with big shivers running over her. Floyd yelled, "My God,
she's havin' a fit, it's a sunstroke!" They all dropped their sacks and
ran toward her. Billie broke out crying.

For a minute, while her whole body jerked and jumped, she fought
at the safety pins that held her big work gloves to her sleeves. Then,
bending low, she caught the bottom of her dress and in one long pull
stripped it up and over her head and flung dress, gloves, and all in a
heap three rows away.

She stood there naked and panting in the beating sun in the middle
of the field while they all, drawn up in a circle around her, stared.
Cleora broke the spell, wailing, "Mamma, not even any drawers on!"
Her nursed-out tits and old-woman's scraggle were bare to the sun.

"Lizard," she panted. "It run up my leg and down my sleeve."

Then they broke into giggles, and Elmo went to pick up her dress, turned it right-side out, and brought it back to her. "Bet you skeered him worse'n he did you," Floyd said. "Skeered me, anyway. Skeeriest sight I ever seen." But Cleora lamented, "Not even drawers, Mamma. What if somebody'd come by on the road?"

They stood in the middle of the field, with the dry white-poufed cotton plants stretching away around them, and laughed at Mamma's having stood naked in the sun, the heat, in plain view of the road, and laughed at Cleora's dismay. Ora Lee whispered to Billie, "Don't it scare you to think of growing up to look like that? Then you'll grow your own weed patch."

But they didn't have many laughs that fall. Work was their reality: hard, gritty work. It was right, Mamma said; it was the Lord's will. "In the sweat of their brow . . ." But Edna Earle reasoned that this was Adam's curse, men's curse, so why should she have to work in the sweat of her brow in the stingy earth? Yet she did not say so, for fear they would tell her she was stiff-necked and sinful. She merely thought it. And besides that, word was the price of cotton would be down even from last year, when the bottom had dropped out, so that even after their laboring was done, they wouldn't make enough to buy what they needed, let alone wanted.

She worked sullenly, and looked and acted sullen, until the brooding look was deeply ingrained and part of her. It wasn't fair. After having the woman's curse and the man's curse, both, to be unable to have any of the things she wanted so! She began to fear she would always be shut out from the store-window world.

III

LATE IN OCTOBER THEY DROVE the blacktop road to Clarksville to settle up for the year. Elmo drove the team with Mamma beside him, straight and starched in her good gray dress and hat, instead of the usual floppy bonnet. Under the seat were jars of preserves and a few eggs she meant to sell; about every two miles she wondered aloud if they were riding all right or if she ought to hold the box on her lap. After great argument, Ora Lee had been allowed to ride up front where she could be seen by town blades. Edna Earle and Cleora and Billie jolted along on the back of the wagon with their feet dangling. Between them and the others the cotton was piled high.

Only Floyd had not come, because it was his day to work at the gas station. He had left that morning in a black fury at missing a Saturday in Clarksville.

It would have been enough to make anyone excited, usually. Billie had been full of herself for days; she couldn't stop talking. But Edna Earle rode along glum and silent, thinking about all the bad things that were bothering her: geometry and the woman's curse and Jake Glover and all their hard work and the price of cotton. It would all be so much better, she reasoned, if Papa (a benevolent man-shaped cloud in her imagination) had not died.

She had looked forward to the new things the cotton money would provide her. She was tired of being an outsider at school, sitting at the edge of the group at lunch, listening in on talk that didn't include her. She had no doubt of the reason: she wasn't one of them; her clothes were not like theirs. She had forestalled discontent by looking forward to this day. But now that the last of the cotton was in, and they were on their way to sell it, Mamma said not to look for much money to spend. Everyone said how the price of cotton was down, how they didn't know how they would make it through. Groups of men had stood around the church door the last Sunday they had service, shaking their heads and discoursing in low tones on the market reports from Memphis and the poor prospects here. As if telling about a death in the family, a particularly scandalous death, they stopped talking and looked off whenever one of the women or children passed.

Riding on the back of the wagon to Clarksville to sell the cotton, Edna Earle puzzled over the strangeness of it all. Until now, she had not thought of her family as poor. They had always had plenty of food—even more than they could use, so that Mamma was forever giving this and that to neighbor families that didn't have as much. Every kind of vegetable you could think of: tomatoes, peas, beans, corn for boiling in summer and for cornmeal all year. Fruit, too: berries and peaches and pears and some knotty apples and even cherries from one tree at a corner of the place. And sorghum and ribbon cane syrup. Mamma killed two hogs every fall and smoked and salted the meat; there were squirrels and rabbits in winter; milk and chicken and eggs, all they wanted. All they ever had to buy was flour, salt, baking powder, a little coffee, a loaf of light bread now and then, for a change, and maybe a piece of tough beef if one of the neighbors killed a steer and came around selling meat. They had two hundred acres, counting cultivated, pasture, and woods, all fenced and cross-fenced the best of any place she knew of. Grew all their own feed for the stock. And a good house, always painted. And the best-cooking, fanciest-scrolled wood range you could think of.

There had never been a lot of cash money, but it always seemed like they had enough. And then something had happened to the price of cotton last year, and now all the men were talking about it being worse this year. It was just unbelievable. There was some mistake. Mamma would be wrong yet, the others would be wrong. After all, here they were driving along the road to Clarksville with a good-sized load of cotton, under a tarp in case of rain. And Floyd had already brought one load over. Mamma had the receipt for it. Edna Earle clenched her fists, willing it to be: a new coat, a bought school dress and a dress-up dress, two pairs of shoes. Maybe it should be a red party dress, and she could dance at the next party.

She wondered if the others were doing the same, willing the money in, thinking of what they wanted. Billie, sitting beside her on the back of the wagon, was swinging her legs and looking at everything they passed. It wouldn't take much to make her happy. And with Cleora, on the other side, you could never tell. She stole a glance at Cleora and, sure enough, she sat there erect and rigid, her little mouth squeezed down and her solemn eyes fixed on the road unwinding from under the wagon. She might be riding along praying. Elmo, driving the wagon, probably *was* praying. Anyway, he wasn't thinking about money and party dresses. Ever since he told them about wanting to be a preacher, he had been like this, moping around, brooding all the time. He had taken to going around with a pinched look that said, "Yes, I know the rest of you have these little wants; don't mind me, I am above them and wrestling with the things of the spirit." It got tiresome after a while.

Ora Lee was a different story. She wanted to be in town and have pretty clothes as much as Edna Earle did. It had been a momentous year for her, too. She had turned seventeen in June, a loudmouth and a cutup, three years out of school. Three or four of the sons of nearby families—Coot Tyre and Billy Clarke and the two Mankins brothers, usually together—had begun to drive by of a Sunday evening in their wagon and offer her a ride to hymn-singing.

There was one particular Sunday evening when she got all spruced up to go, thinking the older Mankins boy would come alone, for once, to drive her to singing. She was such a crazy thing, she always got so excited about things. Mamma said she didn't have a lick of sense. Mamma told her she had to eat something before she left, and she argued and sputtered around, because she didn't want to be eating when he got there, and finally after wasting time arguing she stood by the end of the table and stuffed cornbread into her mouth with her eyes snapping sparks. And of course, hurrying like that, she choked on crumbs. When Tom Mankins, having knocked and got no answer but hearing a commotion inside, stuck his head through the kitchen door, Ora Lee was standing face against the wall clawing it as if to climb it, was climbing it really, while Floyd laughed and whacked her between the shoulder blades. She sputtered and rolled her eyes and let out weird whistling sounds. "My God, she's croaking!" Tom yelled, and he rushed out onto the stoop and snatched up a bucket half full of water and threw it at her, hitting her on the head with the bucket besides half drowning her. Mamma made him leave for swearing, and Ora Lee went down behind the barn and cried for an hour.

Ora Lee was always running full tilt up against frustrations like that. It was a bad time for her. She was cross to Cleora and Billlie. She complained to Mamma about not letting fellows play cards in the house with Floyd and not letting her go to a party one Saturday night at Billy Clarke's cousin's house in Clamie. Whenever she did ride out with someone, after she had come home and gone to bed, Mamma would slip into the room and inspect her drawers by the light of the kerosene lamp in the hall. Edna Earle, pretending to be asleep, would watch her, wondering what she was looking for.

The last Sunday in August Floyd had a fist fight in the churchyard when some fellow twice his size said something about Ora Lee. When the other fellow pulled a knife, all the men jumped in and put a stop to it.

Then, to top things off, Jake Glover resurfaced, and Ora Lee became not merely restless but scared and confused and angry. She sang a daily refrain of dissatisfaction. Mamma hoped Ora Lee would get married soon, but so far nobody seemed inclined to bring that about, and Ora Lee only knew that she wanted some fun. Her plans for the future did not include counting every nickel and doing without things, staying home with Mamma and doing the same work over and over.

So she rode up front, all anticipation, primping her hair and smiling a secretive little smile, and Edna Earle rode on the back, not so much looking to the day in town as looking to what it would get her for later on.

When they arrived at Clarksville they drove straight to the gin. It was early; they had started before daylight. Even so, they found half a dozen wagons in line ahead of them, not counting the one then giving up its cotton to the suction of the pipe. Mamma made the girls stay right there, wouldn't let them wander around and look in the stores until she could go with them, so the wait seemed endless. When the wagon was finally empty, Elmo was sent over to Market Square to try and sell the eggs and preserves—a poor-white effort the family had never before had to make. Meanwhile, Edna Earle stood against the wall in the cotton agent's office, openmouthed, while Mamma settled up, dealing hard and quiet like a man but without a man's routine and expected profanity.

Then suddenly it was over and Mamma was saying, "All right, girls, I guess we might as well get on with it." As she marched out of the office, pulling Billie by the hand, the rest followed. The next stop was the county courthouse, set in the middle of the square, with more cars than wagons circling it in a crowded jumble, entering at one street and veering away at another. Climbing up the big front steps and, once inside, up a flight of stairs, again they waited in line, this time to pay the year's taxes. Mamma dealt with the tax man as grimly, and in as few words, as she had dealt with the cotton agent.

Then it was nearly noon. Sitting in the wagon, they ate lunches Mamma had packed the night before. No one had much to say. Only Mamma knew how much money was left after the taxes, or how much of that she had to hold on to for the rest of the year, but it was plain to them all that things weren't looking good. At last, after they ate, they set out to shop. The broad sidewalks around the courthouse square were crowded with country people like themselves, all trying to figure out what they could best do without. There was less talk, less noise, than usual. No one seemed to have that glad look—not reckless, but as close to reckless as an East Texas dirt farmer ever gets—of crop in and hard work over for a while. Even the popcorn man was doing a poor business, and the man selling balloons outside Woolworth's was waiting till someone stopped to buy before he blew one up. Billie knew better than to ask; even her good cheer was dissolving fast. Men standing on the corners talked in the hushed and solemn tones they had been using all fall. One, holding the Paris newspaper, read aloud about great numbers of men out of work in Dallas and Fort Worth. He shook his head and said, "Times is bad all over."

Their time in the store was a time of frustration and struggle for each to gain at the others' cost—all but Elmo, who said, with a pained and patient look at the holes in his shoes, that he didn't need anything, he could do without. It ended with Ora Lee victorious and Edna Earle in a pout for the red dress that got away. When the three hours of looking and pondering and hard decisions were over and they were back in the lint-lined wagon, with the horses' heads bobbing in front of them on the road home, it was Mamma that was doing without.

They had wheedled and teased and pouted her out of more than she could afford, and they knew it. No one got two pairs of shoes, as they usually did, but everybody except Mamma got one, anyway. Edna Earle had a ready-made dress and material to make another. Ora Lee even got the new coat she had been wanting, got it by staging a yelling and crying fit in front of everyone in the store. Between all of them begging or just looking big-eyed at what they wanted and the clerks saying, "Miz McCall, this is a real good buy, and wouldn't it look purty on the girl?" she didn't stand a chance. But for herself she had bought nothing, not even the dress length she wanted bad, not even knitting yarn to pass the winter evenings, not even a box of snuff. Now she sat with her mouth drawn into a knot of crankiness and worry, and the girls looked sideways at each other, ashamed. The fields they passed looked stripped and barren, in the woods only the pines were green, and the day was all wrong.

IV

IF THEY HAD COME TO TOWN in fearful quiet, they went back home in utter silence, and Edna Earle was almost asleep when Elmo pulled up by the gate. It was dusk. She jumped down and shook herself awake as she ran ahead of the others, between the dry stalks of the summer's flowers, up to the front steps. There she stopped and stood, confounded and trying to grasp what had happened, until the others came up. They seemed a long time coming, and, staring at the porch, she had begun to bawl "Mamma, Mamma," before she realized they were already there and standing stunned like herself.

All the front windows were broken, and the best rocker thrust in pieces through one of them. Half a dozen chickens lay with their necks wrung and their blood smeared around the porch, feathers strewn. Patchy, Billie's cat, was strung up to a nail on the screen door, and the screen wire was cut and pushed out of the frame.

Billie was the first to make a move. Seeing the cat, she ran up to take it down and set up a wail at the first touch of the cold, stiff body. Then they all went up to pull her away. Mamma gathered her in and patted the back of her head. Beside the cat was a note: "I ben hear." "Who, Mamma, who?" Edna Earle cried, but at Mamma's one narrow look she remembered and knew.

Elmo cleaned off the porch while Mamma looked all through the house. Nothing was hurt inside, they thought. Then they came to the front room and saw the big bed there, Mamma's bed. The mattress and quilt were slashed and the mattress stuffing pulled out like spilled guts. Then she spoke for the first time, "My mother made that quilt." She never flinched or cried, only her eyes went a deader gray and her mouth set tighter, as she turned away and went to make a fire in the stove for supper.

Ora Lee ran off to the bedroom in a screeching fit, but the other girls hovered around while she woodenly stirred up cornbread and heated butter beans. Why did he do it? Would he come back? What would he do if he did come back? They all talked at once, on the verge of tears. Mamma only shook her head; she didn't know either, or understand.

Wanting to demand how she could have married a stranger like that
—a man so mean—unable to say it, and yet from the pressure of
resentment unable to keep quiet, Edna Earle burst out that that was
some papa Billie had.

It was too much for Billie. She doubled her hands into fists and
stamped and screamed, "I don't have a papa! I never did, and I won't
have one now! That mean old man! That old turd!"

Mamma slapped her across the face and told her to keep a decent
tongue in her head. Then the only sound in the room was Billie's
snivelling against the door frame and the thumps of Cleora setting
plates on the table. Ora Lee's fit had run its course and they could hear
the clinking of glass from the porch, where Elmo was sweeping up.

Edna Earle edged out of the room and went to watch him. The dead
chickens and cat were gone; only a few dark spots on the wood
marked where their blood had pooled. The pieces of the broken rocker
were stacked against the house. Almost before she noticed, Elmo explained that he was going to try to put it back together.

When he said that he was going on to do the milking, she caught his
arm and begged him not to go. Jake Glover might be hiding in the
barn. Or he might be hiding in the weeds, in the dark, waiting to come
in on them while Elmo was out at the barn. But he flung her off and
told her to leave him alone. "I'm telling you, he's gone," he said. "Now
you'll be all right. Go ahead and eat without me."

She sat on the top step and listened to his footfall fading away into
the darkness. Elmo wasn't very big; if a man jumped on him from
behind, he wouldn't be able to do much about it. The barn loomed up,
a blot against the lesser dark of the sky. Then the lantern came on and
bobbed around inside. Behind the barn the thick pine woods blotted
out everything clear up to the sky. They had never looked so dark or
so near before. Woods all around, shutting them off from everybody,
except on the side where the field, now stubble, rose gradually to the
main road. Anybody could be hiding in those woods. She was glad to
run in when Mamma called that supper was ready.

They sat around a coal-oil lamp in the middle of the table and tried
to eat, looking at each other wide-eyed and at Mamma, who kept her
eyes on her plate and hardly seemed to notice what she did. The lamp
cast their shadows on the walls. Still Elmo did not come in. After a
few minutes the girls got up and cleared away the dishes without any
talk. They were nearly through when Mamma looked up. "Oh," she

said. "I didn't notice you done that. Why don't we just spit-bath tonight and draw up water tomorrow night, instead? I don't reckon we'll go to church tomorrow."

"Fourth Sunday, Mamma," Cleora reminded her. "Preacher won't be there, anyway."

"That's so. Well, go on and . . . wait! What's that?"

They listened hard. A horse was being ridden from the road to the front gate—but then on past the gate and toward the barn, so everyone knew it must be all right, and said so at once. They went on out to the back stoop to wash, and found Elmo there with the milk. "That was Floyd that went by," he said. "I didn't get to talk to him yet."

Edna Earle was still washing when she heard Floyd come in and ask what was going on. Mamma told him in a few words. "He left this pinned on the door," she said. Edna Earle could see again the note, "I ben hear," printed crude and slanting on a torn scrap. How could Mamma be so calm? She wanted to press herself against the wall until she faded into it, so he would never be able to see her and get at her.

When she went in, Floyd was sitting at the table with his hat shoved back on his head. She passed through on her way to the bedroom, where she listened to them while she got into her nightgown. Ora Lee, amazingly enough, had put on a fresh dress and tied up her hair; it was Saturday night, and she was going to sit on the porch.

"Get the cotton sold all right?" Floyd was asking.

"I reckon. Best I could get, anyway."

"Pretty bad, huh? Walter Epps was by the station today and said it was bad."

"Yes, sir, bad is right. Five and a quarter cents. Five and a quarter. I never thought to see that. No, sir, I just don't know."

"Where's supper? I ain't had a thing but a Coke and crackers since breakfast."

That brought her back to herself. "You take your hat off at the table," she told him. "Then I'll get your supper. I kep' it warm."

"Aw, hellfire, Mamma, don't start in at me." He threw the hat through the lean-to door onto his and Elmo's bed and sat in silence while she set out his supper, her mouth set tight. "All right, I won't say it again. Here." He fished in his pocket and pulled out four wadded bills and some change.

She counted it on the table, then looked up at him. "That's four dollars and sixty-three cents," she said. "Where did you get the extra? You been gamblin' on cards?"

"No, Mamma, I ain't been gamblin' on cards. I didn't keep none of the wood-choppin' money except fifty cents, and I had a little left from last week."

She sat down across from him, wiping her hands slowly over and over on a dish towel. Edna Earle thought to herself, watching from a straight chair in the hall, that she looked worn out. Sometimes it came to her like this how hard Mamma worked, doing man's and woman's work both, and for how little return. She wished she could recreate herself somewhere else, somewhere nice, with money, and move Mamma there and buy her things.

"The wood-choppin' money is yours for spending money," Mamma was saying. "A nineteen-year-old boy's got to have somethin' to spend, I know that."

"Take it," he said.

"No, it's rightful yours."

"What do you aim to buy window glass with? What are you goin' to pay the doctor with if anybody gets sick? Or pay for flour and coffee with? Your good looks? Hellfire, Mamma," forgetting his empty promise not to swear, "there just ain't goin' to be enough money this year if Elmo and me don't do somethin'. Cotton down last year, down more this year . . ." He threw down his fork, turned away, and sat with his elbows on his knees.

"Hush, you'll scare the children," she said. Out on the porch Billie was asking if anybody would play checkers. When Ora Lee snapped at her, Elmo went out and said he would.

They heard a car churning through the slough of dust between the turnoff and the gate. Its headlights picked through the house as it turned and then there was a honk. "Hey, Floyd," someone yelled. "You comin'?"

He went out on the porch, and told them not this time.

"Aw, c'mon. You ain't got nothin' to do here."

"Ain't got nothin' to do if I go, neither." Then added, "Nothin' I'd want to stay with you fellas to do, anyway."

They laughed. The one at the wheel was gunning the motor. The one standing on the other side and talking over the top of the car, Alvin Blaymans, said, "Well, if you're sure you ain't comin'."

"Yeah. I'm sure. Whose car?"

"My cousin's, from Paris. That's him drivin'. Well, if you're sure. H'lo, Ora Lee. Hey, what happened to your windows?"

"Oh, nothin' much." And then they were gone. Ora Lee grinned and stirred on the step; her evening's vigil had been worthwhile. Edna Earle leaned out the window to tease her, softly so Mamma wouldn't hear. "D'you see Ora Lee wall her eyes at Alvin Blaymans? Or maybe it was at his cousin with the car."

But Ora Lee was in no mood for teasing. She jumped up and turned on her, eyes sparking. "You shut up, you little twit, or I'll show you what for."

"You better go on to bed, Edna Earle," Elmo told her.

"Girls," Mamma said, "you just leave the boys alone, both of you. You'll have to fool with them soon enough, when you'll wish you didn't."

Floyd went back in and slammed down in his chair again. By the lamplight he cast a heavy, bent shadow on the opposite wall. His shock of light hair, fuzzy like Mamma's, looked wild as he ran his hand through it. He made a couple of passes at his food before resuming their talk. "Mr. Epps wants me to go to three days a week at the gas station, instead of two."

"That right?"

"We could use the money."

"That's a fact," she said. "Won't have near enough canned tomatoes to last the winter, burned up too early in the season. Flour and sugar nearly out now. But I think we'll make it. Got plenty of pork to kill next month."

"Have to get a new bed, new window glass. Need fence wire."

"You better tell him you can't for now. We need you around here."

"He might get somebody else. We could use the money."

"I know it, but we'll make it."

"Well, I could use the money, then!" he exploded. "Them bastards that just come by while ago, they knew the reason I couldn't go was I couldn't hold up my side if I did." He began to pace up and down, into and out of the circle of lamplight. "You and the girls and Elmo can keep the place goin'. Not so much to do now, anyways."

Another car went by, and Floyd went to the door to try to see who it was. He stood there a while kicking his shoe and then said he was tired of staying around home and would Mamma get him another fifty cents of the money he had brought in. When she brought it, he continued to linger and to shuffle his foot. "Maybe if I went out to Fort Worth to Uncle Buford . . ." he said at last.

"No."

"Aw, Mamma, just think. Maybe we ought to all go. The bottom's out of cotton, no money, now old man Glover around, no tellin' what he'll do next."

"No. I said no."

V

SHE SAID NO ALL THROUGH THE FALL and into a mean winter, while more things went wrong than she could count. No every time Floyd said he wanted to go off to Fort Worth to Uncle Buford and get a job. No twice in letters to Buford when he urged her to sell the place and come. No to Ora Lee when she wanted to go to the fair in Paris with Alvin Blaymans' cousin, when she wanted to get her hair curled, when she wanted to live in a room in Clarksville and get a job in the dry goods store or a cafe. No to that even though the ten dollars a month Ora Lee said she could give the family would have made all the difference, what with the cotton money nearly gone before Christmas.

No to Edna Earle when, after two months at school, she said she couldn't get geometry at all and would just have to quit. "I never wanted you to go to that school," she said. "I don't see no use in it. But you started it and you're not a-goin' to quit." So all through the gray chill of late November and into December, on the three days a week that Jess made his milk run into Clamie, Edna Earle waited by the road for him in the darkness of six a.m., jolted into town without a word and then walked up and down the street until the school opened, arriving back home close to eleven hours later, worn out and miserable. And when Mr. Adrian West, her teacher, said he could give her extra help with her studies if she stayed in town during the week and came to school every day, Mamma said no again. And she persisted, even when he said there was an extra room where he was boarding that Edna Earle could have for two dollars a week including board if she would help in the kitchen. Edna Earle went around red-eyed and silent for days after she said no to that.

It was a hard time. Word of Jake Glover's visit got around, and there were days when Billie came home from school crying because the children taunted her about him. They made up a rhyme and sang it at her at lunch time:

No pa at all.
Pa come back in the fall.
Crazy and mean—

Tar him and feather him
And pick him clean.

Mamma tried to tell her it didn't mean anything and she bet Billie could make up a lots better rhyme about their folks. It wasn't much help. "Stick your tongue out at 'em," Ora Lee advised her. "Show 'em you don't care. Or make 'em quit; scratch their eyes out." Billie shook off the tears and tried to laugh about it, but she wasn't the same. She did care.

All kinds of things went wrong. When the weather turned cool, Mamma had Ben Martin come and kill two hogs, and except for some chops they ate that day and the next and the quarter she had to give Ben for butchering, she started the hams smoking and salted down the rest. That was to be their winter's meat. Then, with money so short, she decided to sell the other two shoats. But not a week after they were gone and the money spent on fencing and other necessities, there came a spell of hot weather the like of which nobody had ever seen so late in the year, and somehow after twenty years of salting down pork she hadn't done it right and the whole lot went bad. Even with the boys shooting squirrels pretty regularly (and once, after there was snow on the ground to keep them out of filth, a possum), she had to start killing a laying hen now and then.

Two other things went wrong that unseasonable hot week in November. One of the cows, the best milker, died; they never knew why. And Jake Glover showed up again.

They hadn't heard anything out of him since the day he tacked his note on the door. After two weeks of fearful waiting, she had told them that the mess he made was his revenge on her for sending him back to the state asylum and that now he'd had his revenge he wouldn't have any more reason to stay. Probably he'd cleared out that very night. They all, all but Ora Lee, said things like "That's so," and "Of course, bound to," but no one knew whether to believe that the others believed it. A few times Mamma thought the cornmeal was a little lower than it ought to be, or that there seemed to be a jar or two less of beans or preserves than she remembered, but she was never sure.

Then the Sunday after that week of unseasonable weather had been broken by two days of wind and rain, a Sunday when the sky and earth were one bleak color, they saw him beside the road as they were on their way to church. He had a shotgun, and his pants legs were caked with mud up to the knees. He never appeared to look at them at all as they drove past him, but just to look off at nothing. Billie said, "That was him, wasn't it?" Mamma screwed her mouth tight and looked straight ahead. But Edna Earle looked back. He stood there alone and dishevelled, with his shotgun drooping from the crook of his arm.

At church Hubert Ott sidled up almost shamefaced and asked if old Glover had caused them any more trouble, because he thought he saw him awhile ago at the edge of the woods down the road apiece. "We seen him, too," Mamma said. She knew Hubert had never gotten over feeling bad about being the one to suggest Glover ask her for a job, all those years ago.

The next day, Edna Earle saw him in Clamie while she was waiting for school to open. He was far off at the other end of the street, so that she could make herself believe she wasn't sure she had really recognized him. She didn't tell Mamma. But on Wednesday and again on Friday he was around, appearing at the far end of the street after Jess left her off, or sitting on a pile of cottonseed-hull bags on the loading dock of the feed store as they were driving out of town in the afternoon. Jess had bought an old truck, which enabled him to cover a bigger pick-up and delivery route, and he wasn't used to driving it yet. When she said, "Isn't that old Jake Glover?" he wouldn't look up from his driving, but said he didn't expect it was, because he didn't think old man Glover would be around anymore.

That was the eleventh of December, two weeks before Christmas. On Monday and Wednesday of the next week she went to school afraid. There was no place for her to go between the time Jess dropped her, before seven, and the time the janitor opened the school, a quarter to eight, except the empty street. It was still fairly dark at that hour. She got out of the truck already watching over her shoulder, but Jess never seemed to notice. She wished she could go sit in the cafe, but that was impossible: only the men went there. She planted herself in front of the Montgomery Ward catalog store, where there was a light in the window, and kept watch. On those two mornings the street was empty, and on the way home she didn't see Jake Glover among the stubbled faces of the old men in overalls and jumpers who talked and spat on the feed store dock.

But on Friday morning, exactly a week before Christmas, she saw him loitering behind her, keeping an even distance and crossing or doubling back when she did. There could be no doubt who it was, and on a dark morning, cold and sleeting, it was an uncomfortable certainty to know that a crazy old man, for seven years implacably intent on getting back at them all, was dogging her steps. In school that day Mr. West said pleasantly that it appeared Edna Earle was too excited about Christmas to concentrate on her studies. Any other year it would have been true.

That evening at supper she told everybody that she was through with school because she couldn't get geometry, and when Mamma again said no, she broke out crying and told them about Jake Glover. No, he hadn't done anything or said anything; he was just there, and she knew he was watching her. Elmo wanted to call in the sheriff right then, but Mamma wouldn't. There was no need, she said; what would they tell him, anyway? They could take care of it themselves. Look what they had got into by going to the sheriff the first time. He argued that it was risky to let him keep hanging around Edna Earle, and Ora Lee said what about the rest of them, didn't they matter? But Mamma shook her head; as long as he didn't actually come around again, didn't do them any harm or cause any trouble, they would leave him be. But Edna Earle would quit going to school, that much for sure; there was never any use in her going in the first place, and with all this it was time to quit.

Elmo had to work at Badgett's store the next day, and Floyd at the gas station. They milked and got in plenty of firewood before they left, and Elmo got Mamma to say she and the girls would stay in the house with the doors locked, just in case Jake Glover was hanging around. He had to go away soon, with the weather so cold and, as far as they knew, no place to stay.

It was another dark, overcast day, with occasional flurries of wet snow, the flakes melting against the windows and the porch steps. They moved around listlessly, picking things up and putting them down again, and looking out the windows front and back until nearly noon. Ora Lee complained every few minutes about how tired she was of being shut up in this old house with nothing to do and never any fun.

Mamma just sat, worrying to herself over how to make a decent Christmas. For the moment, all problems had narrowed down to that. Actually, she had worried about it all fall, sensing in some corner of her mind that it would be the last Christmas. She wanted to make it a good one. But how? Finally, along after noon, she said that all this idleness and watching were driving her crazy, and after all Christmas was coming. So she went out to the kitchen and called Cleora to come get the oven fired up while she made a batch of tea cakes. She cut them in stars, and for a while it seemed almost festive to be doing holiday baking, but when they had finished it was only two o'clock and it would be two hours or more till either one of the boys would be home. It seemed that no one passed on the road all day. The girls sat and looked at the Sears and Roebuck catalog and debated which dress was the prettiest and which dishes, which curtains, which hat. Then Mamma remembered she had an old catalog under a box of scraps in the front bedroom, and Billie cut out paper dolls until first Elmo appeared, and then Floyd, shortly before dusk.

No, they hadn't seen a sign of him. No, they hadn't been scared, not a bit. And to Floyd's inevitable question, she wasn't ready to think about selling the place and going to live in Fort Worth like Uncle Buford said.

Sunday was another long and quiet day with no sign of Jake Glover and nothing much to do, once the few chores were done, but sit around. Floyd paced, and shuffled, and slammed in and out. Ora Lee primped and tried fixing her straight hair with twists and pins and ribbons, all the while wishing for this and that. In the evening she went off to singing with the two Mankins boys even though Mamma had said positively she couldn't go. Or anyway she said they were going to singing. It was after twelve o'clock when she came in, let out at the gate by someone in a gray Ford (something the Mankins boys certainly did not possess) who circled and spun off through the dust before she was in the door. Asked what she had to say for herself, she told Mamma she was tired of going to the same old hymn-sing with the likes of them, that might as well be seventy years old for all they knew about having a good time, and with the old horse pooting in her face all the way there and back. Mamma called her a hussy, and Floyd laughed.

On Monday, Elmo and Mamma drove in to Clamie with the best chair, a platform rocker which in a fit of inspiration and surrender she had bargained to sell, tied in the back of the wagon with an old quilt wrapped around it. After Elmo delivered it to old man Badgett's married daughter, he went to tell Mr. West that Edna Earle wouldn't be back, and Mamma did a little shopping with the money from the chair. She had worn her good gray dress and her stiffest posture and tightest set mouth in preparation to confront Jake Glover, but if he was there he never showed himself. On the way out of town she gave in to the prolonged tension and cried into her handkerchief while she clutched on her lap the parcel that represented Christmas. Her crying was a fearful thing. Elmo gripped the reins and stared straight ahead at the road.

On Wednesday the twenty-third, Mr. West came all the way out after school to bring Edna Earle's share of the refreshments from the class Christmas party and a very small gift wrapped in green paper, which he said she should save for Christmas morning. When he drove up she was hanging out clothes in the cold wind, shapeless in Floyd's old jumper and hat. She wanted to burrow into the ground and hide, or turn her head and pretend he had stopped at the wrong house, and that she didn't know him. But he had recognized her, and already Mamma was out on the porch to ask him in, never regarding her spotted apron and the strings of hair that had escaped and now hung every which way. So she had to go in, and take off the wraps, and sit down across from him with her running nose and red hands, and every time he glanced her way she felt branded. He sat at the kitchen table and drank two big cups of the precious coffee while telling them how sorry he was that Edna Earle was leaving and that he was sure she would have made a good pupil if circumstances had allowed her to attend every day and he was sure she would grow up to be just as fine a woman as her mother. At that Edna Earle bit her lip and stole a look at his waving hair and slender hands.

She went off to the front room and cried when he left, and long after his wagon had disappeared she stood looking down the road and fingering her griefs.

At last she put on her old coat and went out to the barn, where Elmo was forking down straw for the stock. It would be a cold night. A few stars already showed pale over the western rim. She followed him around for a minute and asked if he didn't ever wish to get away from there. He wouldn't stop or look at her, but got a little feed for the animals and then said no, he'd miss her and Mamma and the rest too much. "But don't you get tired of all this and want to make something of yourself?" A preacher, he said; she already knew that.

Then he added, "You know what I'd really like? I'd like to have a little church down here, maybe our church, and live in a little house, but nice, you know, with you and Mamma. I'd make enough to live on so we wouldn't have to keep up a farm, just a garden, and you and Mamma could keep house. She'd be old by then, and we could take care of her so she wouldn't have to work hard. Don't that sound nice?"

It didn't, really. She wanted to go live in Clarksville or in Paris or someplace where people had important jobs and houses with rugs on the floor and nice things. She was tired of being country. But she would never be able to make a teacher now, and Mr. West talked like she was just a little girl and not fit for anything. "Yes," she told him, "yes, that does sound nice. That's what we'll do. I'll keep house for you and Mamma, and while she cooks in the afternoon I'll get dressed up and go call on the Sunday school children's mothers, and we'll stay right here always."

"Maybe in the house on the back piece," he suggested. "We could fix it up real nice."

"Yes, and sell all the rest of the place."

"Or rent it."

He was milking then, making the old cow's milk zing and foam in the pail. "Brother Young says I'm comin' along real fine," he told her, with gaps between the phrases timed with his pulls on the teats. He laid his cheek against the cow's flank and looked up at Edna Earle. "He said I'll be ready to preach by Easter, maybe sooner. Hey, look around for eggs, will you?"

She found four, and they walked back to the house together. Elmo sighted a rabbit in the dried and frostbitten remains of the garden. When they stopped to look, it sat up and gazed back at them, as still as it could be. The dark pine woods seemed far away, and a faint smell of Mamma's molasses-and-raisin cookies baking carried even to the edge of the garden. It was like a spell was on everything, just for the moment—a spell of home. Elmo set his milk pail down, shyly touched her arm as if testing to see that she was really solid, and then solemnly kissed her cheek. "You're my best sister," he said.

VI

SHE HAD TO SELL THE BEST CHAIR to Badgett to do it, but she made Christmas. There still wasn't much in the way of presents. Toothbrushes and toothpaste all around, a bottle of sachet for Ora Lee, hair ribbons and a piece of embroidery for Cleora, colors and two coloring books for Billie, wallets for the boys. She had been gathering it up and keeping it hidden all through the fall. On the very day they sold the cotton, she had bought Edna Earle's present. In the belief that her desire to go to high school indicated bookishness, she had chosen a book, *Great American Presidents*, that she had spotted in a store window decorated with a sign that read BACK TO SCHOOL.

All this she had bought from what was left of the cotton money, leaving a small roll of ones and fives in the bottom of her coin purse in case of illness. She spent long hours—while her hands went on shucking corn or liming under the outhouse or mending or kneading—in a stupor of anxiety before the ominous fact that the roll of bills was so small and the time until another crop so long. Even if she took every dollar and half-dollar that the boys made, it didn't look to be enough to get them by. There was nothing to do but take a firm grip and hold on. But she had held on so long!

She never put it to herself in words, this will be the last Christmas we can hold on, but abruptly faced away from that gray wall of sure defeat and, ignoring it, set about making a good Christmas, whatever else would follow. And so in two minutes of dickering on old man Badett's front porch she had struck up a deal to sell the platform rocker, and she spent every bit she got for it on candy, raisins, oranges, cocoa, white sugar, and bright paper and tinsel for decorations.

The day before Christmas she was up in the early dark to start things going. Floyd was working at the gas station from seven to four, and in a last-minute burst of extravagance she gave Ora Lee two dollars from the shrunken roll to go in with him and get her hair cut and fixed in the beauty shop. They left, laughing and scuffling on the wagon seat, in the darkness of six o'clock. While the girls washed dishes and straightened up, Mamma gave the wash pot a final thorough scrubbing, started a fire under it in the wash shed, and as she had every year since Ruth was a baby, started a whole ham to boil. All day, through intermittent rain and wet, melting snow, she slogged between house and shed in a pair of aged work shoes that had belonged to Virgil McCall, to keep the fire right and the ham cooking. As soon as their quick noon meal was cleared away, she took out the decorations, a surprise that they had all hoped would come, and they set about making chains, stars, tinsel wreaths—whatever they could think of. Another quick check on the ham, and she started on yeast bread and fruit pies for tomorrow's dinner, molasses candy, and a 1-2-3-4 cake.

She had never been a real cook. Cooking was an essential chore she had taken on before her teen years, when her mother took to her bed. Through all the years since then—nearly forty, it was—she had cooked, day in, day out, regardless of the field work and barn work and housework there was to do besides, unless she was lying in with another baby. As a regular thing, she took no interest or pleasure in it, but at Christmas and on a few other occasions, cooking took on the joy of festivity. Especially now, for this was to be as fine a Christmas as she could make it, and in the festive ritual of holiday cooking she was able to forget—or at least give no mind to—the small and smaller roll of ones and fives, the impossibly long time until another crop, Ora Lee's wildness and Floyd's restlessness, Jake Glover, who had dropped out of sight again since scaring Edna Earle in the early morning on the main street of Clamie.

When Ora Lee and Floyd got home it was all done. While they washed, she set out a perfunctory supper, the last preliminary to the holiday. Ora Lee was strangely unsettled, lapsing into long silences, chewing her bottom lip, giggling and mimicking the people she had seen in town, but Mamma marked it down to the new hairdo. With it all frizzed up around her face, she did look pretty, in spite of a too-sharp nose and eyes too close together. Cleora said Ora Lee was silly, but the other girls admired her hair and wished they could spend the day in town getting fixed up and looking at everything. They ate fast while the darkness settled in, but even before they had finished it started: people in and out from then till ten o'clock. All the Otts, the Mankins boys snickering in corners with Ora Lee, Alvin Blaymans in for a while, dominoes on the kitchen table, checkers on another. Popcorn and cider, cookies and cocoa, molasses candy and bright hard candies in swirls and pleats that somebody had brought. Mamma won twice at dominoes, the only game she knew, beating two entirely different sets of players, including Janey Byers' father, a wizened, older-than-his-years man, always in striped overalls, tonight clean and starched. Old man Byers was generally conceded to be the domino champion of Cut Hand, some said the champion from Clamie to Talco.

When the Byerses left, Floyd went off after them, and Ora Lee slipped off with Alvin Blaymans in a car, not his, while the second game was going. When she noticed they were gone, Mamma had 215 to Tom Mankins' 180, nobody else close, and while he shuffled she went down the hall to where Billie and the youngest Lewis girl were playing checkers. Yes, they saw Ora Lee leave just a little while ago. Mamma stopped a minute to look out the front door; a car and a wagon were parked outside the gate, and Billy Mankins' horse stood with head down and a back hoof lifted, tied to the sweet gum tree. She went back to the table. It was Christmas Eve; no use making a fuss.

Elmo stayed home all evening, standing with his hands in his pockets or taking a quiet hand in dominoes or passing around the candy bowl. This was how things ought to be, he thought, everyone at home, together. At some folks' houses on Christmas Eve there was moonshine whiskey. Thank the good Lord Mamma would never have any such! How would he ever have heard the calling and made his sacred vocation if there had been that poison around to kill the spirit? Floyd would have brought it in, though, if he could. It was much better this way. He passed a dish of Mamma's molasses candy and managed to grin when someone said if he had a red suit he could be Santa Claus. Tom Mankins shifted his quid and said, "A red suit and about sixty more pounds."

He sat off at one side and watched the party. Yes, this was how Christmas Eve ought to be, everybody at home enjoying Christian fellowship. But that Ora Lee! He frowned and tightened his lips. She had to go slipping off in sin. Satan was after her soul, he was sure of it; he would try to drive Satan out and call her back, only she would never listen to him, never heed God's anointed. To be anointed, anyway, when Brother Young said he was ready. And Cleora, too, for all her pious ways, she was like to fall into the sin of self-righteousness. He longed to say to her, humble your heart, Cleora

Mae McCall. But a prophet in his own country . . .

He thanked the Lord that Edna Earle wasn't like the others. Every night he thanked Him for her. His best sister. They were the closest in age of any of the issue of Mamma's womb, a sign that they would be closest in spirit and she would follow him always, as she had followed him from the womb. And now she had said yes, they would live here together with Mamma and have a ministry in this place. He longed to tell her to give him the hand of commitment and the kiss of holy love.

Oh, she had a spirit to be tamed, he knew that. Sometimes her willfulness rose up and smote her sweetness of temper, and then her black eyes snapped with rebellious self. But her strong disposition made her more worth saving; he would wrestle it to the ground and subdue it. He was glad she had stopped going to the high school. It was good she had wanted to go and learn, but there were snares for her feet there. He had seen that Mr. Adrian West, with his soft hands and beguiling words.

He watched them all and smiled to himself. Mamma did love to play dominoes! He wished she could play more often. He and Edna Earle would live together and take care of Mamma and make things easier for her.

He frowned.

He had been reading the Scriptures with Brother Young, and his mind kept running on Saint Paul: that I would do I do not, and what I would not do I do. It was a hard verse, telling how hard it is for God's anointed to keep to the straight and narrow path that leads aright. Who will deliver me? Paul said. It is better not to marry. He would not marry, he never would. Lord, deliver me from looking on women to lust in my heart. This night of all nights, Christmas Eve. Janey Byers, and the little Mankins girl, not much older than Cleora but with . . . He would live with Mamma and Edna Earle and never marry. Better not to marry. But better to marry than to burn. Did any of God's other anointed ever burn, or was it only himself? When he lay on his back at night beside Floyd, when Floyd was asleep and snoring, and threw off the covers and his member rose by itself and throbbed and his breath came tight. Was that burning? In the moonlight it looked as big as his whole body. Or did Paul mean the burning would be later on, burning in hell if when it rose by itself unasked he took it in his hand? Because ministers are supposed to think on things of the spirit. When he lay awake at night he thought other things; that was burning. Once he had stood in the door of the girls' room at night, watching them—her—sleep, and pumped it till it gushed sticky into his hand and he had to go out and wash. It would be better not to burn, but what could he do?

He sat meekly, watching the others. Edna Earle was playing hide-the-button, an innocent game. They would never have guessed. Old Sobersides, Ora Lee called him when she came back in, just as the last visitors were drifting off, long before Floyd came in. She went right on to bed, still hectic and still baiting Cleora, but drawn, dishevelled, with a glaze of fatigue over her joking eyes. It had been a long day.

Elmo sat and read the Christmas story in the Bible. He had wanted them to ask him to read it out loud, but they had all gone on to bed. It was just as well; he would have blushed and stammered. After they had all gone on, only Mamma left sitting, he asked, "You comin' to bed, Mamma?" But she wrapped an apron around her shoulders and carried a chair out to the porch.

Used to sitting there through summer evenings, she noticed the winter quiet. The stars themselves, showing between ragged clouds, seemed no quieter than the woods. That was one good thing about the place—plenty of woods, no lack of firewood. It was a good place, a sight better than most of the places around. Grew everything. Oh, not melons so much—old man Byers always grew the best melons— but pretty near everything. What had happened to cotton, to money? They might still tough it out and hang on to the place. If only the young-uns didn't push so hard to go off. An owl hooted way in the pines toward the bottom. She shivered. There came Floyd up the road. Better go in and not seem to be out here just watching for him. Thank the Lord Jake Glover hadn't been around.

Christmas morning they all scooted around: eating a light breakfast, milking, getting the chickens fed. Before they knew it, Ruth and Jess and the baby were pulling up and crowding in to thaw by the fire. At last, they opened their presents. Mamma had made the baby a rag doll, and Ruth and Jess gave him a rubber cat and a ball. He was crawling now, and he pushed his pretties around, trailing the front of his dress around the floor till it was black. All day, they took turns keeping him out of the fire. Elmo had bought Mamma a jar of snuff, and Floyd gave her a brooch. Cleora had hemmed her two handkerchiefs with FDM embroidered in the corners. Ruth brought her several skeins of yarn, which was a way of bringing gifts to everyone, since she would knit in the winter evenings until her hands cramped, making vests and scarves for them all. Everyone looked to see what it was that Mr. West had brought Edna Earle, and when it was only a bookmark no one knew what to say until Ruth said wasn't it pretty and Edna Earle put it in the exact middle of the book Mamma had given her, where it remained, never marking a place in a book never read.

For Mamma, Christmas was the biggest day of the year. After the Christmas Eve cooking there wasn't much to do but heat everything up and make her special sugar pies, a kind of custard as sweet as their name. Ruth had brought candied yams and a jar of green beans. So she spent the rest of the morning dozing in a rocker by the fire with her big, knobby hands slackly folded, for once, in her lap. Then after the big dinner, when the table was cleared and Ruth said she and the girls would do the dishes, Mamma got Jess and the boys into another big domino game, playing to 500 and then to 500 twice more, with the bones clacking on the tabletop over the rattle of the dishes and little spurts of talk and laughter when, twice, young folks drifted by to see Floyd. Once Alvin Blaymans stuck his head in and joked about gambling. "This ain't no gambling game, and you know it," she told him. "I won't have no cards nor no gambling inside this house, and you know that, too." But he said all he knew was she was settin' there playin' a gambling game and he had half a mind to get some boys and start up some poker right then and there in the front room, only—he winked at Ora Lee—he wouldn't want to get a mean old lady like her mad at him.

She called him a feisty thing and told him to take his smart mouth and git, but she laughed, too, and said to tell his folks merry Christmas.

When the last game was over, Elmo put the dominoes back in the box while Ruth and Jess gathered up to go home. "You sure are a good player, Mamma," he told her, glad to brag on her a little.

"I swan, I could play dominoes all day and all night if I had a chance. It's been too good a day to be over with."

Ruth and Jess left, and then Floyd, too, probably gone to see Janey Byers. She got out *Saint Elmo*, by Augusta Jane Evans, her favorite—actually her only—book, and read the first chapter before it got dark.

She read solemnly, and shook her head over the unregenerate sinner, secure in her foreknowledge of his redemption by the influence of the heroine, Edna Earle. "You know, Edna Earle," she said, "when you was born I had the awfullest time choosing between Augusta Jane and Edna Earle for you. I felt like Augusta Jane was too put-on."

But Edna Earle was looking into the window, which was beginning to reflect the just-lit lamp, and at her own form against its backdrop of gathering dusk. "What was it like when our Daddy was here?" she asked.

"You don't remember him. I know you don't. You couldn't. You was such a little thing when he went." She paused a minute, looking back to that time. "Well, he was a fine man, your Daddy was, a good worker, a regular churchgoer. He always loved Christmas, too. That was his favorite time."

Cleora, reading her nightly chapter, looked up to ask what it meant in the Bible when it said "the Virgin Mary." Mamma explained that meant she was a young girl, that all young girls were virgins, and Cleora went back to her reading, happy in the thought of her own wonderful virginity.

Edna Earle kept her gaze at the window. Having been at the high school, she knew there was something more to it than that. She had never spoken about such matters to Mamma. Until one day in the barn, when Mamma had sent her to look for eggs, she had not even known how baby things came to the world, and Mamma would have whipped her for watching it. She remembered that day so well. Just as she stepped inside, she heard an awful bellow out of one of the cows. She saw the animal on the floor, its sides heaving and its big eyes rolling up, with a big bloody bubble just sliding out between its back legs. She stood astounded while the cow licked over the awful, wet thing until there emerged distinctly a little splotched calf. Then the cow looked at her gravely, and she remembered to glance around for eggs before running outside and standing for a minute to catch her breath. So that's how it happened!

But she couldn't confess to Mamma that she had intruded on the cow and seen this monstrous thing. No, Mamma would be mad at her; she knew that instinctively. She had been so careful to bring them up right and keep them away from the things that some of the girls whispered about at school. Just this fall, Edna Earle had begun to think she understood when a girl at lunch said, "Well, what do you think people keep bulls for, silly?" Mamma had always been very careful, taking her time, keeping things hidden away and secret.

Then Mamma put *Saint Elmo* in the bottom bureau drawer and set out the remains of the pies for a snack supper, while a big pot of coffee perked on the stove. After they ate and she cleared away, she got a skein of the maroon yarn that Ruth had brought and cast on a vest for Floyd. While Billie colored three pictures in her new books and Elmo, whittling on a hickory stick in the shadowy corner, looked up at all their faces from time to time and whistled tunelessly, she spent the long evening knitting and, when her hands began to cramp, luxuriously, improvidently, drinking cup after cup of rich strong coffee, yellow with cream.

And still she sat, long after Ora Lee surprised her by stopping to kiss her and say good night before trailing after the others to bed. She sat until the fire was burned down, the coffee gone, and the vest front up so far you could see the points of the first row of diamonds.

It's been a good family Christmas after all, the very thing. It's nice being here all together like this. It's real nice. All but Floyd, anyways. He sure goes off a lot lately. Musta been to see that Janey Byers again. He sure hangs around her enough. But nobody came by to get him to go anywhere so it musta been there. Blamed if I can see what he sees in her, little mealymouthed thing, not enough gumption to . . . jist walks meencie-meencie with those little bitty steps. Well. They get it in their head to take out after a girl there's no stoppin' 'em. Wonder when Elmo'll take the notion. There he sets, lookin' a thousand miles away except when he remembers we're here and looks at us for a minute. Not a word. Reckon he'll make a preacher sure enough, always settin' away off like that. Maybe that'll keep him from chasin'. Wonder why they have to get that notion anyways, why they can't jist let it alone. They can't, though. Girls just as bad, though, some of 'em. Thank the Lord mine ain't. Cleora askin' what's a virgin! Ora Lee don't have a lick of sense, seems like. I hope she don't make a fool of herself like some of these gals do. Well, if their Daddy could see it he'd be right proud of how they've turned out so far. Been careful as a body could be, kep' everthing of that kind outa the way. Ha'n't been easy at times. Law, no. Had to take the old cow away down behind the woods to the small house place to let old Lewis's bull come, keep 'em all away during the time. Life woulda been a sight easier if Virgil

*hadn't died, poor thing. Wouldn't a-done to make a to-do over Ora
Lee kissin' me good night. She wouldn't never again if I had. She's a
good gal really—they're all good—just not a lick o'sense sometimes, it
seems like. Yes, sir, it woulda been a sight easier life all these years if
their Daddy had been here. Some days I thought I'd never get through,
draggin' young-uns around, plowin', everthing a woman ever had to
do and all a man's work besides. Just had to tough it out, that's all.
Been purty tough, too. Poor old Virgil, just worked hisself to death.
He was a good husband. A good provider. But I ha'n't missed havin' a
man foolin' around all the time. All that nuisance. Why the good Lord
made it so people had to go through all that to get babies . . . And
then the poor women gets all the suffering and then all the work of
takin' care of 'em; all the men has is their pleasure. Virgil never was
nasty about it, though. Not like he coulda been. Not till later,
anyways. Poor Ruth. She does have to put up with it. Says that Jess is
after her all the time. Comes up to her in the kitchen sometimes with
the thing already out and in his hand. Phoo. My land, what an awful
nuisance. She just has to tough it out, too, do her duty like the Bible
says. Oh, I can still call to mind how it was at first, after we got over
bein' strangers. A while after the first one died, and from then on till
after Ruth was born and then till I was carryin' Floyd. It wa'n't so bad
then. I had pleasure of it, too, nearly like Virgil had, I guess. No
shame in that. He woulda been ashamed of me, I expect, if I'd told
him. Never did. But after Floyd was born, and they was two to look
after, and then Ora Lee so soon, it was just one more thing to do, like
haulin' water. He got nasty about it then. Or shamed. Musta been
thinkin' all the time there'd be more young-uns. Just muscle in and
poke and snort. Talk awful sometimes, even. Why can't they jist let it
alone? Seems like they can't, though. Well, I couldn't a-stood a old
man at me. Jist fumble, fumble, all the time, they say. So I never had
to. The poor thing, that spring he died, and he knew he was, and he
tried to figger what I best do to get along, all of us, without him. It like
to drove him crazy, right here in this bed. But Jess ain't a bad man,
he's good to Ruth. Virgil always did love to set in the evenin', ever-
body together like we done this evenin', always loved checkers, not so
much dominoes, I always beat. Always loved Christmas the best of
any man I ever knew of. He woulda liked today. It was a good
Christmas. Thought we wouldn't have ary a thing, but I made it a
good Christmas. The last one, maybe. Oh, the fire's nearly down. I*

hate this day to be over. Lord only knows if we'll be here next Christmas, or where we'll be. I'll do three or four more rows. Wonder what that Floyd is up to. If he could get more days at the fillin' station and if Elmo could maybe pick up somethin' else to do we might hold out. I don't know. Then when it come time for spring work, where would we be? I done it all once, before they was big enough to help, but I can't again. Maybe so we could fix up the rent house a little and move into it and rent out this one and the most of the land. Maybe so I'll write to Buford and see what he thinks. Don't know who'd rent it, who'd have the money. Who'd want it, for that matter, though they had ought to. It's a good place. I been through a lot here. I swan, I don't know how I could leave. Still Floyd not in. I hope he ain't up to nastiness. Got to figger out somethin' and keep us together. If I can just do that. Plague take that Jake Glover! How I could ever a-married him, and it Virgil's own bed at that. Billie's a sweet thing. I wouldn't a-missed her for anything. If he'll just stay gone now. It was a good Christmas anyway. Hate to go to sleep and leave it.

VII

ORA LEE disappeared the night after Christmas.

Looking back, they realized that they should have seen it coming, should have but didn't, in her silences and tension and even in her brief tenderness to Mamma on Christmas night. On the day after Christmas she stood in glooms or flung herself through hateful tasks with an angry momentum that knocked things over and broke dishes. That night, when she paused on the way to bed, a chance word from Cleora set off her temper and she retired in slams and crying.

In bed she turned toward Edna Earle. "All these times I've been riding out with fellows," she said, "I guess you've been wishing I'd take you along." She hadn't even thought about it, she said. "I should have, though. I should've thought to." Edna Earle didn't know about that. "Don't you want to do something besides stay here and feed the chickens?" She did, oh, she did. Still, something about Ora Lee made her uneasy, almost scared her.

The next morning Ora Lee was gone, she and her clothes and a shopping bag from Leonard's Department Store in Clarksville. She had left a note pinned to her pillow: "Dont come after me, dont worry, I am with Ronald, we're going to get married."

Mamma waved the note in their faces and demanded to know who was this Ronald. They knew. It was Alvin Blaymans' cousin. She was too distraught to do anything, but Ruth came for a couple of days and Floyd got a ride to Paris Monday morning with old man Tyre. There he stomped between the sheriff's office and the newspaper office all afternoon, and the next day he thumbed his way to Clarksville and did the same thing there. But the only thing he accomplished was the placing of an ad in the personals column of both papers and the spending of money they couldn't spare. There wasn't a trace of her, and nobody that he could find who had the power to marry people had married them.

After that, Mamma spent her days, when she wasn't dragging through her work, sitting by the front window with her right elbow in the palm of her left hand and her forehead resting in her open right hand, staring at no one knew what in the dust of the floor. She talked to the Blaymanses and wrote to Buford. Once she even had Floyd take her in to Clamie so she could make long-distance telephone calls to the sheriffs in Clarksville and Paris, and then to the police station in Dallas, and finally to Buford in Fort Worth. More money gone for nothing.

Edna Earle bided her time. She would get out, but not like this.

On the day after New Year's, a gray, raw, blowing day, Floyd was up early to go to work at Walter Epps's filling station, and Mamma was up to get his breakfast. Ora Lee had been gone a week, and Floyd had already said let go of it, let her go. But Mamma wouldn't let go. Now she wanted him to go that day and see the Blaymanses' kin again and see if they hadn't heard something. He said he wouldn't do another thing about that girl, she was gone and good riddance, they ought to let her be. In the morning darkness they shouted at each other in whispers across the table, so as not to rouse the others.

Until Floyd hissed at her to let him alone about it, damn it, let him alone about everything, and stomped out to leave. But his eye lit on the woodpile. It was low, and the day was cold. Mamma would be onto him again, saying he left too much for Elmo to do. "She won't leave anybody alone," he muttered. "Has to boss everything, has to have everything just so. Shit, no wonder Ora Lee run off." Fetching the axe, he started to chop and split some wood before he left. It was still nearly dark, he was fighting mad; the axe went wrong.

It was lucky he didn't cut off his foot and bleed to death right there. Actually, the blow was only a little off target; it was more a matter of his failing to take a firm grip, so that the handle turned and the blade hit his foot a glancing blow. He yelled for Mamma while he hopped and lunged toward the house with the blood spurting, and for a few minutes she was everywhere, yelling for Elmo and fixing a tourniquet and rags to soak the blood and trying to hitch the team, then running back to throw a coat over her gown and wrapper while Elmo hitched up and got Floyd into the wagon. They drove him into Clamie as fast as possible—faster—with blood getting all over them. The doctor said if it had been much longer Floyd would have bled to death, sure enough. As it was, he took forty stitches to close the foot and said he guessed they could take him home but bring him back in five days, and keep him off his foot for a couple of weeks.

It wasn't till they got back home and calmed the girls that they thought what the accident meant in money. Two weeks, the doctor said. That meant he couldn't go to work, and they had counted on what he made at the gas station just to get by. The doctor would be five dollars, maybe ten, and there was no question of asking him to wait. The McCalls had never done that. She got out the roll of bills. That would leave only thirty. There was no way they could keep going for long without what Floyd brought in. As soon as they came up against that realization, Elmo saddled up and rode back in to ask Walter Epps if he could switch around his schedule with old man Badgett and work both jobs, but Epps didn't want him.

It turned out even worse than they expected. The foot got infected and Floyd had to stay two days at the doctor's to fight the red streaks that had started down his ankle. The doctor's bill was twenty dollars. Floyd had to have a new pair of shoes, and he was laid up three weeks instead of two and lost his job.

There was no way out but to move into the rent house, the small unpainted house that stood on a back stretch of the property, separated from the main farm by the woods. At one time the rent house had brought in a nice little income, but there hadn't been a tenant in it for years, and no one had even been around to see what shape it was in for maybe a year or more. They could move into it, and rent out the main place. Maybe they could, if they could find somebody to take it. That was the only answer they could think of.

Mamma had seen which way the wind was setting a week after the accident, when they had to take Floyd back with infection. While she was in Clamie she stopped by the feed store and asked Ben Martin if he knew of anybody looking to rent a place or if he would watch for someone. Three days later, Jim Russell, a bachelor tractor dealer in Clarksville, acquainted with Martin through business, pulled up at their gate and asked if they were the folks wanting to rent out their place. She wanted to say no and turn away, evade the fact, but how could she, with all of them gathered around, watching her, listening, knowing as well as she did what a tight spot they were in and wanting to go. Floyd sat in the front room in the repaired rocker, his foot propped on the side of her bed, ready to take over the dealing if she should falter. So she opened the door narrowly and showed the tractor dealer to a chair in the center hall. In five minutes they had come to terms, with Russell to take over whenever they could get moved. Then he was through talking. He stood, minutely nodded his head in lieu of a handshake, put his hat carefully in place, and left.

Billie, imagining a family moving in, intercepted him at the door to ask how many children he had and did he think they would like the place. He stood plainly baffled for a minute, but offed with his hat in habitual politeness to even a child woman. Then comprehension spread on his face. "Oh, I ain't going to live here myself," he explained. "Maybe my man that runs these places for me. Ma'am." He nodded again and left.

"So it ain't good enough for him even to think about livin' on it," Floyd said. "Hell, he couldn't even figger out what Billie was talkin' about. I guess he just runs all them extra tractors from one place to another all over half the county and sets there in Clarksville rakin' in the money. That's the way they do it, while the likes of us works our butts off for nothin'."

"Well, he don't look to make much out of this place," Elmo said. "Not unless he knows some way around the market price that we don't."

"Them big dogs always knows a way around it, that or anything else," Mamma burst out, with a vehemence that surprised them, the momentary overflow of all that sour discouragement that had been filling her up for months. "Plague *take* it," pounding the harsh rhythm with her fists on the door facing, "*them* and their *money* and their *offices*, thinkin' they're such big *dogs*. And we can't even figger out how to stay on our own place." She lowered her forehead onto her hand for a minute and shook her head.

"Oh well," she said, after a while. "He seemed like a good enough man. We can't fuss. That's what we said we wanted, was someone to rent the place. So now we got it." Then she lapsed back into the silence that meant she was inwardly fretting about Ora Lee's defection.

She got a fire going in the stove and during the long afternoon ironed some clothes Cleora had sprinkled down that morning. Elmo went out to the barn to shell some corn he would grind the next day at Badgett's. Her iron was still thumping on the board when it darkened toward evening, and Edna Earle took over the rest of the ironing while she went to get something on for supper. They ate without talking, until she broke the silence to tell Elmo he better go around to the rent house first chance he got and see what needed doing before they started moving.

It was on the nineteenth, a clear and thawing Tuesday, that he went. The house, with its few leaning sheds that served for a barn, sat in the middle of a small patch of land surrounded by pine woods. It was a plain double cabin with the dog-run closed in to form a six-foot wide dead-end hall running from front to back. It stood cold and run down, but not quite desolate. If Elmo had been taking notice, he would have seen that. There were signs: the rags clinging in the windows despite the winter wind, the weeds trodden flat by the porch. In the wagon he had some boards, a hammer, some nails. He tied the reins right to the porch rail to have everything handy while he went in to take a look.

That was when he found Jake Glover, who they had thought— hoped—was gone. He stepped through the door and heard the voice and knew whose it had to be even before his eyes had adjusted to let him see that anyone was there.

"I seen you comin'," Glover said. "I knowed you was bound to come sometime. I been watchin'."

Stunned, Elmo stood staring for a minute, already, either by instinct or by the conditioning of long uneasiness, looking around for the shotgun the old man had been carrying the day they saw him by the road. It was in the far left corner, behind him, and in another corner was an old quilt on top of some rags, marking the place where he had bedded. Food, half a cooked rabbit and some corn bread and a jar of preserves, was collected as if for display on the hearth, but the fireplace was black and cold. A strong odor of urine hung in the air. Glover was unshaven and wild-looking, his shoes and pants legs, as before, caked with mud.

It didn't take him long to see that much, not as long as to collect his thoughts and ask, "How long you been squattin' here?"

"A while. Before your sister quit goin' to the school. I thought I'd like to settle near my own flesh and blood. The little girl's right smart lookin', ain't she?"

"How is it we never seen smoke? I see you been cookin'."

"Sometimes I make a little fire back in the woods for a squirrel or a chicken. Or rabbit. I got that-un yesterday. Twice I made up a fire late in the night, when I knowed you'd be all asleep."

"Well, you'll have to get out now. You can't stay here, not anymore. Go back to where your people are, they'll take care of you."

"You're my people, and you been takin' care of me just fine." He grinned jaggedly. "Eggs, a handful of cornmeal now and then, scraps of this and that from the kitchen. Tell your Maw she's a real fine cook to this day."

It gave him the creeps. He yelled. "You git now, Glover, you hear me? You git. You can't have this house. You can't stay around botherin' us no more. Now I mean it." The veins of his neck were working, and he shifted quickly from foot to foot almost in a dance. With the last words, he wagged an unaccustomed fist at the old man, who seemed to enjoy the show.

"Oh, I couldn't do that," he said. "I'd miss you all too bad. I already been missin' seein' that sister o' yours that was goin' to the school. She's right nice to look at, makes a man want to see more."

Then Glover was on the floor, uncut because Elmo was so unpracticed a fighter, but winded and surprised. "I can't forgive you that," Elmo yelled down at him. "I done forgive you everything, like the Bible says. Don't make me have to not forgive you. You keep your mouth shut about her." He started to bend down to his weasel-like adversary, to hit him again, and drew back his right, but dropped it and turned and broke for the door. "You git, now," he yelled back. "You git today or I'll have the sheriff on you."

He drove back home shivering. He had sinned the sin of anger.

Glover did get out, that very night. But first he set fire to the house. They saw the glow above the pines soon after dark, and even though a slow rain had already started and they got there quick with tarps and a bucket for the bucketless well (with Floyd, who still moved painfully, pulling and lowering), it was too badly damaged for them to be able to think any longer about moving into it. And that had been the last way open to them. When they drove back home, they all knew that it was over.

Mamma sat up the rest of the night, staring into the burned-down embers in the fireplace, while Elmo came every little while to beg her to go to bed and the girls, huddled all together, turned fitfully in their sleep, still afraid. In the gray of early morning she lay down on top of the covers and dozed until, in full daylight and later than any of them remembered ever having slept, the others began to wake up. Then, with her face and clothes still smudged and her hair coming unknotted and hanging in variegated strings, she cooked them a recklessly sumptuous breakfast, a feast.

They ate in uneasy quiet. Cleora had dressed and slicked her hair into neat braids, and now, realizing it was after time for school, she rolled her eyes from one to another, not daring to ask what to do about it. Billie took an extra biscuit and left the table, nibbling it dry. Soon the *punk* of her jacks ball sounded from the front room, and Cleora, still uneasy about school, went to take up some hemming. Still they sat in silence. Mamma poured herself more coffee, saucered it, and slowly began to drink it down, with her eyes on the cup.

"Well?" Floyd demanded.

She passed her palm over her eyes and forehead. "Edna Earle, you come wash up here. Elmo, you go milk and take care of things out there. I'll write to Buford now, and when I get done with that we'll drive in to Clarksville to see that Mr. Russell."

"I'm workin' at Badgett's today, in the afternoon, remember."

"Not today. We'll circle by and tell him he'll have to do without."

"Wait a minute, Mamma," Floyd put in. "Just because I lost my job ain't no reason to get Elmo's lost, too."

"I said, he can't go. We all better be together for this. You, too, sore foot or not. Get on with the dishes, Edna Earle."

"Can't I get Cleora to help? There's so many of 'em."

"Just let her alone now. Them girls got enough worries for their young years. You do, too, I know it. But you're closer to grown up than they are. My oldest girl at home now. So you just let her alone for now and wade into 'em yourself."

"What are you goin' to tell Russell, Mamma?"

"I know what she damn well better tell him."

"Floyd, you mind your tongue. I'll just tell him how it is. Maybe he'll want to buy it outright instead of only renting."

So then it was said, but still Floyd insisted on having it nailed down. "You mean, and us move to Fort Worth?"

"I reckon so. I don't see ary a way out."

Edna Earle put down a stack of plates and forks and capered around the kitchen. "Whoo-pee!" she squealed. "We're moving to Fort Worth! Billie? Cleora? You hear?"

"You need not romp around about it, old girl. You may see the day you're sorry you ever left this place. Go on, now, all of you. I got to write Buford."

"Wait, Mamma," said Elmo. "While we're in Clarksville we're goin' by the sheriff's and report Jake Glover burnin' the house, ain't we?"

She turned her back, going after pencil and paper, and just shook her head.

"Damn it all, Mamma, he's right. What all do you aim to let that old man get away with?"

"No sheriff. He hears we told the sheriff, no tellin' what he'll do. He's a crazy man, that's all there is to it. He ain't hurt us yet—"

"Ain't hurt us!" Floyd moaned.

"—but he might if we did that. Anyway, I don't want no sheriff nosin' around, and all this gettin' out."

She sat an hour over her pad of ruled linen-weave dime-store paper. Twice she called Floyd to come put a point on the pencil. Then she folded up the single sheet she had written, put it into an envelope that was printed in the corner "After Five Days Return To," and addressed it. She put on her good dress, smoothed her hair without bothering to take it down and start over, and called everybody to get going.

It was a bitter and wearying road to Clarksville that day.

Russell, the tractor dealer, said he wasn't interested in buying them out and didn't have the money if he was. They made a dozen other stops in Clarksville and on the way home, asking if people were interested, spreading the word that the place was for sale. But who was going to buy a farm with cotton prices gone bust and banks closed everywhere? They went in desperation for three weeks, cutting back, not spending a penny if they could help it. No store bread, no coffee, no sugar. Buford wrote to hold out for a buyer, not to come till the place was sold. When she read them that, Floyd asked bitterly, "What does he think we're tryin' to do, go to lumberin' it?"

Then in mid-February Russell turned up at their door, as if he had been passing and just stopped on impulse. With their price already pushed down by the situation in general and by their own particular fear, he offered them half of that because, he said, he hated to see good folks stuck there, when they wanted so bad to get moved. Mamma had Floyd drive her into Clamie late that afternoon so she could telephone Buford on the doctor's phone after work hours to ask if he would come handle the dealing and the papers for her. He wouldn't. So they mailed him a copy of the sales contract that Russell had filled in on their kitchen table, expecting he would say turn it down.

"Take it," he wrote back. "You ain't going to do any better. But just make him put in there that you keep the mineral rights. They might find oil there sometime. Keep the mineral rights even if you have to take less for it."

So they told Russell it was a deal. But at the last minute it was decided that Elmo would stay on the little place, the rent place. That came about in Russell's office when they went to sign the papers. Mamma surprised not only Russell but everyone else as well (the whole family, even to Jess and Ruth and the baby, had gone to witness it) by demanding not only mineral rights but the ten acres around the rent houses too. She read the whole contract from "Know by these presents, I, Florence Druecilla Guthrie McCall, a feme sole, do sell and convey" to "witnessed under my hand this 24th day of February, 1932" and said, "No, sir, it's been ours all these years, it was Virgil's father's before it came to him, and we got to keep some of it."

Elmo had never wanted to leave anyway, except that he wanted to stay with Mamma and Edna Earle. Belatedly, he started rebuilding the small house, now only a single cabin, one room and a lean-to, and he was to stay with Ruth and Jess until he could finish it and move in. He was taking the cow and heifer, too, the team, two pigs, the few chickens that hadn't been eaten, the plow, the wagon, the shotgun. There he could grow a patch of corn and vegetables, enough to keep himself going with the milk and eggs and with what he made from Badgett, and he could keep studying in the evenings until Brother Young thought he was ready to start preaching. He had hoped to move up the date of his first sermon, so Mamma and the others could be there, but Brother Young had said no, because you don't rush the calling.

On the Saturday evening of March 12, Uncle Buford drove into their yard in a pickup, with another man following in a car. "This here's Bill Quitlin," he said. "He's my neighbor. He said he'd come along and give us a hand for just two dollars and the price of gas. Now let's look around and see how much we got to load. We got to get gone from here by tomorrow noon."

They made it by two o'clock. For the last three hours, Buford muttered and cussed around the toothpick he perpetually chewed because they weren't on schedule. He wanted to leave everything behind, it seemed, just pack up the family and walk away from it all. Mamma had to argue and beg over every familiar object, and she won in most cases, but not in the case of the stove or the kitchen safes. "Kitchen safes, Florence! Godamighty! They have cabinets built against the walls now. I ain't about to haul them old things."

Elmo took the stove and one safe.

When the pickup was all loaded and a tarp tied over, they wandered through the house while Buford sweated to be gone. It was strewn with objects abandoned or overlooked, here a sunbonnet, there a few hairpins, on top of the rejected kitchen safe a coal-oil lamp, half full. In the bedroom corner were the unused remants of a tablet and two pencil stubs, left from the school supplies Elmo had bought Edna Earle for her birthday, now so long ago. She pushed them this way and that with the toe of her shoe while Mamma finished one last check. It was good, she thought, to be getting away from this tacky old place. She wouldn't need pencils and tablets; she would get herself a hairdo and clothes and do something better, get a job and have fellows that wouldn't think she was no better than a farm girl like Mamma. She could see the barn through the bedroom window, but it didn't call her back with any fondess. Only, for just an instant, there came the image of that calf just borning. She shook herself. She was glad to be getting away.

Billie had found a lost crayon and two checkers, and ran out with them to Uncle Buford's neighbor's car. Cleora stood solemnly at the door. "Mamma's ready now," she announced.

Some of the neighbors had come by during the last couple of days to wish them well, the Tyres, Hubert Ott, the Eppses, Mrs. Clarke and Billy. But now there was only Elmo to say goodbye. He kissed them all, and told Edna Earle he guessed this meant giving up that idea of her and Mamma keeping house with him when he got to be a preacher. But she hardly listened to him. That idea was at the far end of her memory, with brighter prospects pushing it out.

"Unless you decide to come back," he added.

VIII

THEY HAD BEEN IN FORT WORTH a month when the first letter came from Elmo: he had had the laying on of hands, he had preached, he had moved into the house.

The second letter came a month later: "Don't be scared," he wrote, "but bad news. I am in the county jail at Clarksville. I shot Jake Glover. He come in the store and said something he should not. I had already done tried to forgive him. He is dead. I guess this does me for a preacher. Dont come. I mean it. I dont want you to. I guess they will send me to Huntsville. Mamma, Im sorry."

She sent Floyd, thumbing his way, to do what he could, which was precisely nothing (except to bring Janey Byers back with him), for Elmo would give no explanation.

He had stood by the gate that day they pulled out in Buford's truck and the neighbor's car, going to Fort Worth. He had stood there unwaving and had watched after them until they turned on the blacktop. When there was no longer even any trailing dust cloud to watch they were gone indeed. The quiet settled around him. Still he didn't go on, but sat on the front steps until dark, not so much expecting they would turn back and drive up, as expecting they would reappear, simply resume their places, and things would go along the way they always had. He went in and slept on the floor, and in the morning he milked and ate a little from one of the jars Mamma had left, and went back to sit on the steps.

On the second day Ruth sent Jess to see why he hadn't shown up, and together they got his stock moved to what was his place now and Jess brought him back to stay with them for a while.

It took him another week or more to get the house fixed up to where Ruth would let him move into it. She said, "Elmo, there's no call for you to go over there where it's not fit for a human to live in, when we can give you a pallet and meals a little longer." But he was glad when he could go on without making a fuss and his days could fall into their own shape. He had his chickens and stock to tend to and his garden to get ready for planting. He read for the ministry with Brother Young, and he went back to clerking for old Badgett the same as before. Sometimes he took the shotgun and kept it under the counter so he could make out to do a little hunting on the way in and coming back.

Except for Brother Young, the only time he saw anyone, to talk to, was while he was at the store, and then he only said hello and yes he'd heard from the family or no he hadn't. He did what he needed to around his place and then sat by his door. All the time he thought about Mamma and the girls, or actually about Edna Earle. He didn't think about them the way he used to, but only—with a kind of stubborn fatality, his mind running over and over the same deepening worn circle—about their being gone. He wasn't bothered any more by thinking about other girls, women, either. Better to marry than to burn, Paul said; he read it over and over. But he no longer burned. His flesh was numb; it didn't bother him with its stirring and rising anymore.

When he thought about Mamma and Edna Earle he thought, too, about Jake Glover. He repeated to himself the mumbled formula of forgiveness and God's love and his own Christian concern for the old man's soul, but he hated him with a fixed and implacable hate. It was clear to him beyond doubt that Glover—not the Depression and the price of cotton or any other thing—had driven Edna Earle away. One part of him prayed for saving grace for the old devil, and one part prayed, over and over, oh, God, damn him to hell.

Glover turned up again one day when Elmo was at work in the store. He had just weighed out two pounds of sugar and was adding up the total when he heard the bell on the door and looked up to see Glover coming in. Elmo had thought he was long gone, after the fire, and was so surprised that he didn't say a word, just stood there. Grinning, rubbing his stubble, Glover said, "So they all taken off. Didn't say a word, just up and went and taken my little girl with 'em. I sure hate that. A man's got a right to be around his own young-un."

There was no one else in the place then. The customer had left, and old man Badgett was out back, puttering around with something when he was supposed to be resting. Elmo stood and stared at him and thought, God, how ugly he is. His clothes were dirty and rumpled, and he had a greasy, shapeless hat crammed over his head. A grin like a possum's showed his teeth, dark and snaggled.

Glover leaned over the counter, his stale whiskey breath in Elmo's face, and in a harsh whisper said, "What I really hate is they took that other one off, too, that blackheaded one with the pert little ass. I was countin' on gettin' a little piece of that. Didn't you ever look at that and think about gettin' up there and—"

That was as far as he got. Elmo took up the shotgun, his father's shotgun, from under the counter and shot from the hip, a direct blast that left Glover's middle like chopped meat.

But Elmo never told anybody how it happened. To do that, he would have had to repeat what Glover said, and that he would never do. He would only say that Glover deserved to die, and he did the Lord's work in killing him. "Give me Huntsville for it if you want to," he told the judge, "but I done the Lord's work." Years later, though, when he was out and living in the little place again, he would sit with his bottle and think about it. "Nastiness, always nastiness," he would say, to no one at all, because there was never anyone there. "Just the same old nastiness, always the same." He would slip through the woods and spy around Ruth and Jess's place and around the old home place, sunk in ruin as it was, keeping watch over them.

For Mamma, Elmo's crime was the crown and seal of the tragedy of the move from home to town. For her that two-hundred-mile trip was a disaster, a journey to captivity in Egypt, a death. A slow death, certainly, a protracted one which would see her from her fifty years when she traveled that road of exile to the seventy-six years of its ending; still, a death, a dying, the shrivelling of her own life as it had meant life to her.

The house they came to was perhaps better than the old house, more modern at any rate. But it was not hers, and it was crowded and unhealthy—with Buford's family and his wife's brother and her own brood, now with a daughter-in-law too, crowded into half enough space—and on a narrow lot. There was an indoor bathroom, to be sure; no more outhouse to walk to in the rain, to sanitize with powdered lime. Instead, an indoor bathroom, the toilet bowl slimy with residue and brown with rust stain.

She never tried to make a garden. The ground was rocky and inhospitable as she walked over it to the grocery store to buy pale vegetables in cans and such newfangled foods as bananas and rice. The jars of snuff she recognized: Garrett's, Honest, Copenhagen. She indulged her urge now, in spite of short money. Why not?

When they were sick with what the doctor called chicken pox (but no doctor ever imposed a three-week quarantine for a mere chicken pox), no neighbors called by to help out, and there were no chickens out back to come off their roost in the morning and fly over the sick ones, and thereby work a quick cure, as every country woman she ever knew believed they would.

IX

FOR EDNA EARLE, it may have been the same road, but it was a different journey. She had sat in the back seat of Buford's neighbor's car with her face against the glass and her mouth hanging open, watching every mile slip up and away. Her thoughts had all run forward, not backward. The things she would have—the boyfriends she would attract, and spurn! Her little black eyes glittered with the thought of it.

She soon learned that it wasn't that easy. In a crowded frame house, with Buford dropping veiled hints for them to pay more and his wife whining about youngsters underfoot, with her favorite brother not only left behind but then actually locked away in the state prison, and her dress-up shoes starting to split along the soles, how was a girl to go on believing in gain and glory? Someone was always coming along to beat on the bathroom door when she was in the tub, fantasizing her plain, straight body into impregnable allure. Mamma promised they would get a place of their own. "Soon," she said. But there was no way. They stayed on at Buford's.

It was the Depression. For a long time Floyd went out every day looking for work. No luck. Finally he took to sitting in the house most of the time, while the money from the home place slipped away. When his and Janey's baby was born dead, he left and joined the Navy.

"Two gone," Edna Earle thought. "Three, counting Elmo." It was as if they were dead. No word from any of them, and she couldn't even imagine them going on someplace else. Especially Ora Lee: it was as if she had fallen down a well, into emptiness. Would she fall away like that, too?

Soon after her sixteenth birthday, she found occasional work at a five-and-dime, then a steady job at Penney's. There she moved around—notions one day, boys' clothing the next, housewares another. She helped people look for what they wanted and sent their money whooshing through air tubes in little rubber-cushioned canisters to the awesome and forever faceless cashiers far away. On her breaks she toured longingly past merchandise she couldn't buy.

She started work in two nice print dresses Mamma made her, and at first when she noticed how the other girls looked at her she thought they were envious. But she began to feel uneasy. They looked so different; she couldn't put her finger on what it was. She began to understand when she overheard remarks, giggles. "Don't you mind them, honey," one of the older women told her. "They never learned any manners." But she didn't want them to have need of any manners when they looked at her. She just wanted to be right.

She began to watch the others more closely, what they wore and how they moved their hands, their facial expressions. At lunch, holding herself apart, she stood on the sidewalk against the store building and watched the office girls pass with their little clutch bags, talking fast and laughing and laying their hands on their friends' arms. She observed the customers, the ones who could pay out a little money without wincing. The first few dollars she could save up went for material for a pongee sheath, then a black skirt and two blouses. She had Cleora make them for her, not Mamma. It was Mamma's fault she had gone to work looking so country in the first place.

Out of every week's nine dollars she gave Mamma six dollars and fifty cents. With that and what the Navy sent every month for Floyd, the little bit Cleora got for helping out a seamstress in the neighborhood, the dimes and quarters Billie earned for little odd jobs, and a little each month out of the money from the sale of the home place, they were able to move into a duplex to themselves. They were coming up in the world. Or they might, if only Mamma wouldn't go out shopping or gossiping in her old sack dresses and sunbonnets, with her stockings falling down around her ankles. It was the despair of Edna Earle's life. Mamma marked herself and marked all of them as the wrong kind of people, country people.

At nineteen she became one of the faceless cashiers herself, making twelve dollars a week and hoarding every penny of what she kept back, to buy something nice now and then. For by now she had a sharp eye for what was good and could distinguish it from what marked its wearer as one of the worthless. It was her greatest happiness, after passing up the bright cheap things that the other girls bought every week, to use her saved-up ten dollars for a good dress from a sale rack. It might be too old for her, or too dressy, but she wasn't buying her good things for work anyway. She was satisfied with thinking about them hanging at home in her closet.

It wasn't just clothes she had learned from watching the other girls, either. She developed a personality, a knack for making quick, satiric remarks or mimicking people's peculiarities to get a laugh. When young men were around—and they were always hanging around the groups of working girls or churchgoers—she made these jibes for them, looking at each one of them as if he were the only person alive for her just then. She drew off boys from the other girls to herself. There were so many of them and they were so idle; they hung about the Penney's employee door at lunchtime and sat on the duplex porch at night. They took her to the movies when they could afford it (fifteen cents apiece) or to "fellowship" at one church or another when they couldn't. Because she was always alert, always watching, noticing—people, magazine covers, shop windows—she always had something to say. And so her young men thought how clever she was, how sharp, how much sharper than they were themselves. And that drew them, too. They wanted to smash her cleverness, to humble her to their maleness.

If there were two couples or even three—but no one had a living room big enough for more—they danced to radio music, swapping partners without preference but always walking home with the same ones they'd started out with. She warned Cleora and Billie about that, and about not letting them tell the wrong kind of jokes, and about not sitting close.

There were always boys for her; she never lacked. Mamma shook her head and warned. "You better watch it, old girl. These boys can get you in trouble." But she knew what she was doing. She gave them a tidy kiss on the third date, always the third, never sooner, and they never waited beyond that. But if they backed her against the porch and began to breathe hard and go slack in arm and leg, she drew away and laughed as if they had played some silly joke. And if she felt their hands under her skirt or at the front of her blouse, she became angry and insulted. So, in steady succession, her boyfriends went off to others; she never went out with anyone for long. But in steady succession they came back, circling around the well-hoarded prize.

She liked them. They played and clowned and admired her; they were good-looking, as young men certainly ought to be. But they were a shiftless and temporizing lot. Even if they worked hard, even if they kept jobs and made pretty good money, they were, in her eyes, shiftless, because they spent that money on fun—her fun, true enough—instead of saving it. They would never have a thing.

So she stayed at Penney's and kept a sharp eye out for a floorwalker or a buyer, someone with real prospects. But he never seemed to turn up. The floorwalkers she knew were all fifty-two and married.

Ora Lee reappeared with a hangdog look and not much to say. Edna Earle was inclined to resent Mamma's taking her back in without even a fuss; she would have made sure Ora Lee knew she was there as a returned prodigal and had better be properly penitential. But she enjoyed looking at Ora Lee and thinking how much better she had done herself. For a while things were quiet; Ora Lee helped around the house and behaved herself and sized things up, waiting for Mamma to lay down the law, wondering why she didn't. She was biding her time, and Edna Earle, watching her, was biding hers. But when Ora Lee started running around again, things had to be said; she couldn't be expected to stand by and let this happen again without a word. It would hurt her chances, all their chances. So she spoke up, and Ora Lee called her a goody-goody and a snot, and for a while they did not speak. Edna Earle told herself she didn't care. Mamma grumbled a little, and sighed, and lapsed into if not imperviousness at least the semblance of it. She wasn't up to any more emphatic response; Ora Lee would be Ora Lee.

Things drifted along. Floyd, still in the Navy but stateside now, moved Janey away to Baltimore and dropped out of touch. Cleora finished high school and settled into a church secretaryship. Billie developed an eye for the boys and had to be watched. Still no luck for Edna Earle.

In the fall of 1939, when the economy was improving, Edna Earle was twenty-three years old and needing to make a move before it was too late. She began to look for another job and, by luck and the logic of work experience, became a bank teller. That was how she met E. Z. One of the other tellers had an older brother, and he had an unmarried friend, and that was E. Z. Trumbull.

E. Z. was not the kind of fellow who had been seeing her to movies and living room dances, and at first she made jokes about him to the other girls at the bank. He was no dancer at all, big footed and slow, would rather sit and listen to music than dance and didn't even care what he was listening to, just about anything would do. When they rented bicycles in the park on Sunday afternoon, he rode so stiff, as if it was just another job he had to do and a job he wasn't very good at anyway. And his hair standing every which way and him never noticing! And a stamp collection—would you believe it!

But after she had been seeing him off and on for a few months she stopped making fun of him and began to think it might be a good idea to exert herself a bit. She had observed the way he went to work on things Mamma needed done—not skillfully, clumsily in fact—but at least doing them, not putting them off or evading them as Uncle Buford did or as Floyd would have done if he'd been there. She had observed his hunger for a household and regular meals and a woman to keep things going. She had noted the inexpensiveness of his habits, and she was clever enough to realize that inexpensive habits, though they might not be fun in a date, might be advantageous in a husband. He had a steady income, and if he didn't spend it on sailor hats and Victrola records and movies, and if he had no mother to support, where did that money go? Into a bank account, naturally.

Edna Earle was not a wicked girl. If she had disliked E. Z., if he had been a drinker or an atheist or a Catholic, someone who violated her moral standards, she would not have married him. If she had felt any particular antipathy toward him, beyond her antipathy toward the male sex in general, she would not have encouraged him. Neither of these was true. Love? What was that? Doting on a curly-haired schoolteacher who thought you were nothing but a dumb farm girl. She would never moon around after anyone like that again. Certainly love had nothing to do with roving hands and hard breathing. If she grimaced into the darkness of their bedroom when he did the things she had to put up with, if her arm stiffened when he wanted her to put her hand on it, what reason was there to think she would have felt any different with any other man?

And if E. Z. was disappointed, he kept it to himself. What did he know about women, after all? Maybe the books he had checked out from the public library lied, maybe they were all like this. Things might have turned out better, he thought, if she hadn't been so determined to have her mother and Cleora and Billie move in with them to share expenses. What could he expect when, as she often pointed out, her own mother was there to hear any noise they made? But she was intent on saving their money for a house of their own and furniture. She was intent, too, on keeping her eye on Billie. It was bad enough to have one Ora Lee in the family, she couldn't face two, and Billie needed a firm hand. So she got her way: they all moved together and she continued working and Mamma kept house. And it was shortly after the move that E. Z. quit his Civil Service job and went on the road, selling.

When Edna Earle was pregnant at last, they all made a trip down home for Homecoming. That was the first E. Z. even knew about Elmo. She was afraid he wouldn't marry her if he heard she had a brother in the state prison, and she got so used to keeping the secret that she kept it for years after they married. Elmo was out now and tending a little patch of corn and some chickens back in the woods, on his corner of the old home place. Actually, that was why Edna Earle cooked up the trip, to welcome him back from that place they never mentioned and where no one had ever visited him. And it was a good time to do it, before she got tied down with a baby.

If they had expected their visit to lift Elmo's spirits, they miscalculated. Mamma was weepy the whole time, just from seeing old places again, and between that and the sight of Edna Earle with a husband and a swelling belly, Elmo, more taciturn than ever, was driven into total gloom. It was a puzzle to them all, but then, who could ever figure Elmo? Yet E. Z. took a liking to him after all, the way he'd always had a particular liking for Billie.

When the baby was born, Edna Earle's life moved around a new center. Rather, it was as if the center she'd had all along now had a name and a body and a new motive force. She named the baby for Loretta Young, the actress. On Lori she fastened—along with an endless succession of ruffled dresses and Margaret O'Brien curls—all her old urges for respectability and coming up in the world. On her tenth wedding anniversary Edna Earle could congratulate herself on having everything just like she wanted it: a neat house and furniture, a husband who wasn't around the house enough to be a nuisance, Mamma settled in a little apartment, Cleora married off to a preacher, and Billie not absolutely gone bad. And the most docile, tidy girl-child she could wish. For her anniversary present she got E. Z. to buy her a satin down-comforter to keep folded on the foot of the bed—not purple, which she now realized was a gaudy color, but a nice dusty rose.

Part II

I

THERE WAS A GROCERY CARTON full of old pictures on the floor of the back bedroom closet under her mother's out-of-season dresses. She had always known it was there, but until a year or so ago she hadn't paid any attention to it. They were just a lot of old pictures, boring. But now, on bad days or whenever she felt like it, she liked to drag them out into the half-light of the closet doorway and spend most of an afternoon going through them. Mostly there were snapshots, a few studio pictures.

Part of her pleasure in going through the picture box was her awareness that it didn't entirely please her mother. Edna Earle didn't like for her to go off to herself so much. She would have preferred for Lori to be out making herself popular. But how much sense did that make? When you are fourteen and too tall and angular, all oblongs and knobs, and you just know that everybody thinks you're dumb and clumsy and weird, how are you going to get out there and make yourself popular?

Through a long sultry Sunday afternoon, the first day of July, Lori sat in the doorway of the closet, turning through the old pictures of family and relatives and other people whose names she could never keep straight. In the next room her father lay on the made-up bed with his shoes off and a towel under his head, reading a biography of Jefferson Davis. All afternoon, while she looked at the pictures, she could hear the pages turning.

The pictures lay in orderly layers which she was careful to preserve. At the top were the recent ones, the uninteresting ones, mostly of herself looking too tall and clumsy and straggly-haired; in the next stratum she appeared shorter and plumper but no less uneasy, in thin cuffed sox and ruffled blouses; digging deeper, regressing back through hair ribbons and sashes and fingers held up over birthday cakes, she excavated back to fat babyhood. Then there was an album, her baby book, bearing on its front page the hand-lettered inscription, "Loretta Alice Trumbull, June 18, 1942." Her mother was fond of telling people that she had been named for Loretta Young. "And when you grow up," she liked to say, "you're going to be beautiful and rich and famous, just like her."

Just under the baby pictures were her mother and father, newly married or not yet married, with one or another of the couples they had chummed with then, her mother in limp gabardine dresses and curls, her father in white pleated pants with suspenders, straw hat, and, yes, a smile. Then, below these, her mother dressed up and cloche-hatted, with other girls just like her or silly looking boyfriends.

While Lori was looking at pictures, her mother and Mamaw finished the noon dishes, and spent the afternoon sitting in rusty lawn chairs in the shade of the garage, near the flowering pomegranate bush, shelling peas. Lori had already gone out once with a question about one of her own pictures. Now, coming across a picture of her mother between two clowning young men in sailor hats and striped jackets, she went out again. The heavy heat of gathering thunderstorms filled the yard.

Edna Earle laughed, remembering. "Oh, that's Sweetie and Sammy Russell," she said. "Those two! They lived around the corner from us the first house we ever had to ourselves in Fort Worth. A duplex. I was going with them when I met your Daddy. Do you remember them, Mamma?"

Mamaw laughed quietly and shook her head, as peas continued to pelter the gathering cone under her hands. "The silliest two that ever lived."

"Sammy was awful silly," Edna Earle admitted. With her wrist, she pushed back a bit of damp hair and smiled. "Sweetie was the best dancer! I always wished so bad that your Daddy could dance."

Lori took back the picture and went in. Why did she have to talk about him that way? As if it mattered that he was not like the charming Sweetie, who had probably never once read the biography of a great man. She and Mamaw were always talking about him behind his back like that, snickering at his absentmindedness or his lack of skill with tools, or making veiled jokes she couldn't understand. She remembered last Thanksgiving, when the two of them were working in the kitchen. Her mother had held up the curving red turkey neck that she was fixing to boil with the giblets and said, "That looks like something else I've seen a few times," and Mamaw said harshly, "Oh, Lord!" They hadn't known they were being overheard. Hearing, she had realized what the something else was and turned away, her face burning.

Now, coming in from the yard where they had run him down again, she paused outside the bedroom door where he lay reading, but the turn of a page reminded her that his attention was occupied. She didn't really have anything to say anyway. He was gone so much—he represented a line of children's pajamas and T-shirts over a four-state territory; a *four-state* territory, her mother liked to tell people—and when he was away she thought of things she wanted to ask him, but when he came home she forgot them or let them pass.

Now Lori was into a lower stratum where the pictures were yellowed and faded and the people dowdy, their faces running to strange extremes of glee or grimness. She turned through them slowly. Old men and women in high collars stared gravely out from their pasteboard mountings, shutting up inside themselves their secret humanity, while towheaded youngsters in overalls grinned past pet kittens and ducks, and groups posed joyously beside tinny old cars.

She went to her mother with one of these, a picture of a lanky middle-aged man in loose khakis and a straw hat, hugging a dark-eyed and curly-haired younger woman in splashy print dress in front of a model A Ford. The man had a cigar tilted rakishly up between his teeth, and the woman was laughing at him, or maybe laughing at the idea of hugging for the camera. Wasn't that Aunt Ora Lee and her husband, the one that got killed?

Edna Earle answered with an edge. "Oh, yes, of course it is. Don't you get tired of looking at those old pictures? Go on and put 'em away now."

"Let me see it, honey." Her grandmother took the picture and held it up at a slant near her left eye. Then she shook her head and sighed. "Good old Clyde Moody. I never will understand why she done him like she did."

Lori knew the outlines of Aunt Ora Lee's story. Even when they were still living down in the country she had been a wild girl. At fourteen, though bright, Lori was not entirely sure what being a wild girl involved, but she knew it had something to do with boys. Ora Lee had married this man in the picture some time after they all moved to Fort Worth, and had had a baby. But he was killed in a car wreck on his way to California to get Ora Lee—though why she would have been way out there Lori had no idea. Then at some later time Ora Lee had married again, a man named Marvin Elkins who had been happily playing guitar in a western band until she found him and reformed him, having reformed herself some time before.

There in the snapshot Ora Lee was shapely and plump. In the old family portrait, Lori's favorite picture of all, she was a little girl of ten with pigtails, wiry and wild-eyed. Now, or the last time Lori saw her anyway, she was gray, gaunt, over-rouged, and loud. For some reason, but Lori did not know what it was, she and Mama didn't get along. She could remember other abrupt changes of the subject when Aunt Ora Lee was mentioned. She could even remember a scene between Mama and Uncle Floyd over the issue of Ora Lee, something she had done or something one of them had said about her. Others had taken sides. But the details of it all had been kept quiet.

Well, there was to be a family picnic on Wednesday, the Fourth of July. Aunt Ora Lee might be there. She would see.

She put the snapshot of Ora Lee and Clyde Moody back in its place and turned all the rest over on their faces to get down to the old family portrait. She sat against the door frame holding it by its edges, her fingertip hovering over each face in turn, looking for her own likeness to one or another of them. There again were Mamaw and the whole family, Mama and her brothers and sisters, her own problematic aunts and uncles.

Mamaw sat on a straight wooden chair in the middle, holding Aunt Billie, maybe a year old, on her lap. To Mamaw's left, just behind her left shoulder, was Aunt Ora Lee, pop eyes blaring defiance. Near Mamaw's left knee was Mama, Edna Earle, no more than eight years old. At Mamaw's right side, hands resting chin-high on the corner of the high chair back and thin jaws set, was Aunt Cleora. Behind the chair and slightly to the left were the uncles, Floyd and Elmo. In lone shirtwaist grandeur at the other side stood the oldest, Aunt Ruth. The McCall family, all of them together, in this one photograph and nowhere or ever else. It was dated, in spidery pencil on the back, 1925.

The family was all there as complete as it could be with no grandfather, no bearded and solemn, lean man with the band of his collarless shirt buttoned tight—that was how Lori imagined him—to take his place at Mamaw's right hand. When she first saw the family portrait, years ago, she didn't even notice his absence. Mamaw, alone with all those children: to Lori, she had always been alone. Later, when a disposition to notice things and ask questions had begun to emerge, she asked her mother and was told, in a way that implied she should have known all along, that Grandfather McCall had died when she, Edna Earle, was not even four years old. It seemed to Lori very sad to have suffered so great a loss as a grandfather's death, so long before she even came to know of it. Only later, as she came to certain realizations which her mother had tried to suppress, had she thought to ask about Aunt Billie: "But she's more than four years younger than you, I can tell by the picture." Leaving unspoken the great knowledge implied in the question. "She wasn't our papa's," Mama had said, and turned back to her ironing in a way that forestalled conversation.

Lori thought then that she understood the picture better, and her grandmother's tight-lipped expression. Really, it was the first time she had thought about its needing to be understood. It must have been very hard, she thought, to look after so many with no husband. She asked Mamaw about that one Friday when she was spending the night at her little apartment with the worn linoleum and the chamber pot under the bed.

"Hard, I reckon it was hard," she said. "I looked after 'em when they was sick, no doctor around. Plowed, kep' up the place, got the cotton in and sold, chopped the wood, till Floyd was big enough, and then Elmo, or when they was too ornery . . ." And she looked back toward the bone-deep ache at the end of the days, the despair from the black wall of the pine woods of those times reaching across the field toward her, yet she couldn't convey the pain, her words inadequate to bridge the years.

Since then, Lori had sometimes searched her grandmother's long and sagging face for traces of that gaunt woman in the picture who plowed the field and took the cotton to the gin and raised seven children unaided. She searched the picture in turn for signs of the dim-eyed, slovenly old woman, now more than seventy, who had taken her by the hand and walked her to the five-and-dime to buy coloring books and paper dolls. It was hard to harmonize the two, to connect the one image with the other.

In the family portrait Mamaw looked clean, strong, grim. She wore a dark-colored dress buttoned in a band at the neck, with narrow sleeves down to the big-boned wrists with long hands that rested uneasily in her lap. Her long, irregular nose was not yet startlingly humped and drooping at the tip, nor her big ears pendent-lobed; her rectangular face looked merely lean, not hollow-cheeked and flabby-jawed. She was a tall woman, even yet, an inch or so taller than Lori's own five feet eight inches, and in the picture, even sitting down, she looked it. But now she sat by the front window of an ancient two-room apartment on Hemphill Street and spat snuff juice into a coffee can lined with toilet paper. Aunt Ruth, so proud and handsome in the portrait, was the only one of the aunts who was as tall as Mamaw. Until recently she had still lived near the old home place in Red River County in a paintless house Lori had seen maybe three times in her life.

The next oldest, Floyd, lived in Fort Worth and worked at the Convair plant, but they hardly ever saw him. Mama said he was full of meanness, and in the picture he looked it, with his black snapping eyes and a grin just playing around his mouth, his baggy pants and buttoned-up gray shirt, standing cross-legged and leaning on his elbow on Mamaw's chair, a boy of twelve. Then there was Ora Lee again, then Elmo, just a year or so younger.

There she stopped. Elmo, having stood for his picture with his face down, didn't show up too well. She held the portrait closer, but still couldn't see him clearly. He was a little shorter than Floyd; actually neither of them was tall. "Runty," Mama called them. Lori wished Uncle Elmo would come to the Fourth of July picnic, but he probably wouldn't. He was the only one besides Aunt Ruth who still lived in the country, "down home." He lived alone in a two-room house on a ragged piece of land bordered by the piney woods. Lori had last seen him three years ago when they went to East Texas for the funeral of Aunt Ruth's oldest boy, Virgil, who was burned so badly in a fire at the fireworks plant where he worked that they couldn't open the casket. It would be nice if Uncle Elmo came to the picnic, but they didn't expect he would, especially since Aunt Ruth had written that they shouldn't expect her and Jess, and if Elmo came it would have to be with them. Lori liked his downcast face in the picture, with its shadows, and three years ago she had liked his pale eyes and his gray straw hat that he forgot to take off for meals. No one ever talked about him, but Mamaw called him "poor Elmo" and Mama wrote to him at Christmas every year. Why? She had never heard them talk of his having any bad luck, as they did of the others.

One year younger than Elmo, the round-faced child with small dark eyes and stiff black hair was Edna Earle. Yes, she could believe the child in the picture was her mother—that child with hands primly together, standing drawn up as if to hold herself apart from the others, her black eyes staring dissatisfaction at the camera. Something in the stand of her collar told that she had tried to make herself spruce for the picture.

Then there was Cleora, thin-lipped and pigtailed and freckled, a little girl of five in the picture, now red-headed Aunt Cleora. She would be at the picnic, of course, because she lived in Fort Worth and always kept up with family matters. Aunt Cleora could be fun, with her sharp comments and her bird voice and hopping gait. If she hadn't married a minister and settled near Seminary Hill (the Holy Mount, her father called it) she might have been more fun. Here she was in the picture, looking sharply and confidently ahead with her dress buttoned up all neat and her arms straight at her sides. Couldn't they have guessed even then that she would be a preacher's wife and tried to do something about it?

Last was Billie, the baby sister of the family, with no eyes at all because Aunt Billie had punched them out with a straight pin years ago. She said it was because she was such an ugly baby. That couldn't have been true, of course—not Aunt Billie, so pretty and lively, Lori's favorite of them all. It was only one of her pranks. She was full of them, always happy and laughing and teasing Mamaw out of her grumpy spells. Lori hoped so that she looked most like Aunt Billie; she tried to persuade herself that she did, or would. There was a way Aunt Billie had of listening to whatever they were telling her, Mama or Mamaw, and then tossing her red hair back and going ahead anyway with however she wanted to do it, whatever it was, yet not making them mad at her. She always looked glad about things; Mama always looked like she couldn't make up her mind whether to be glad or not.

Lori lifted her head to rub her stiff neck and realized suddenly that the room had been getting steadily darker, a strange bluish dark that had almost obscured the picture in her hands. She had been remembering it as much as seeing it. It was only five o'clock. A storm was gathering for sure. She could hear thunder now and see occasional flashes without even looking at the window. Sweating in the heavy heat that closed in ahead of the wind, she gathered the pictures into the box in order and shoved them back into their closet corner under Mama's dresses.

Just as the heavy rain hit, her father appeared in the bedroom door with his hair standing crazy from lying on it, still holding the book, with one finger marking his place. He pulled back the curtain and looked out at the rain, coming slanted and thick. The sycamore tree in front was tossing, and twigs already littered all the yards. "Where's your mother?" he asked.

"Gone to take Mamaw home, I guess."

They stood together by the window for a while, watching the rain.

II

I T ALWAYS SEEMED TO LORI that she had spent her whole childhood sitting on the yellow-speckled kitchen floor, coloring, while her mother and grandmother talked-talked-talked. On and on, hashing and rehashing all the family happenings of the past twenty years, considering and reconsidering every decision, wise or no, every turn of luck, good or bad. Her head would be down; she would be absorbed in her coloring, staying inside all the lines, making no grass pink and no faces blue. She wouldn't be listening, their voices no more than a droning in the background. But their talk would wash around her and soak in, and store itself up inside her.

Conversation tended to run on food. There were paeans to gardens and fruit trees fifteen or twenty years gone; epics of the great bouts of cooking for birthdays or Christmas. "We grew just about everything," Edna Earle would say—ignoring for the moment all her grievances and remembering only the good parts—"every kind of vegetable we knew anything about, watermelons sometimes, peaches. There were blackberries all over the place in the spring." "We had everthing we wanted, till that dad-blamed Depression." " You always salted down two hogs in the fall." "The woods was full of squirrel. The boys brung home lots of squirrel in the fall, and rabbits, some."

At other times they talked about their hard work, and a note of pride would creep into their voices. They would hurl it at Lori like an accusation: when had *she* ever had to do what they did? It's not true, she would think. They couldn't have, not all that. Anyway, how would they have known how to do all those things? "No man to do the heavy work," Mamaw would be saying, "did it all myself. I seen days I thought I couldn't set one foot in front of the other, but it was out to the cotton field and back to get dinner and out to the garden all afternoon in the hot sun, back to get supper. Cut wood, mend fences, butcher, can. Get the cotton in and sold." Lori pictured her bigger than life, hard muscled, eyes narrowed against the sun, heroic. No, she said to herself. It couldn't have been like that. She knew that anyway it wasn't like that now. She had been there and seen it for herself.

She remembered a trip when she was nine. They had all gone to Aunt Ruth's to attend Homecoming, a daylong session of preaching and singing and communal eating on the grounds of the Methodist Church. Foolishly, she had gone imagining a place of adventure having no tangent to her everyday world, a place out of frontier times. Instead there was a fat old horse, so big she had to climb onto it from a truck fender, that she rode at a walk around and around Aunt Ruth's house. The grown-ups lingering around the littered dinner table looked out through the open window and laughed at her. "Ride 'em, cowgirl!" they said. Through the window she could see the corner whatnot shelf with spindles made of thread spools. She looked at it as she passed, avoiding their faces. At night, sitting on the front porch with the pine woods standing black and final across the pasture, they talked about Elmo's two shoats and Floyd's new truck. When Mama and Aunt Ruth went down the back path with her before bedtime they said there might be snakes, she better stop and squat right there to go. It was easy for them, natural, but she hated it, all of them right there together and seeing and them making fun of her awkwardness.

The next morning Aunt Ruth's younger boys, her cousins, sitting jeaned and shirtless on the front steps when she came out before breakfast, made jokes about the old horse standing off by the fence across the road. "You know, Duane, I'm worried about that horse." "Why, Randy?" "I'm afraid he's got the sticky stomach." She had no idea what it was, black and curving about a foot under his belly. But she knew they knew and they were making fun of her. She knew, too, by sure instinct, that what they were saying wasn't very nice.

That was East Texas to her: shabbiness, coarseness, but at the same time a dimension of knowledge from which she was shut out. She didn't want to listen to all of Mamaw's talk about it. It was boring, and she had no use for it. It made her cross, the way they kept on and on. Still, she managed to fool around with something nearby when they were talking about their times back home.

The best days were when Aunt Billie was there, too—pretty and bouncy and jolly, sitting at the kitchen table with a Coke, laughing at some nonsense or other while they did whatever it was they were doing and talked-talked-talked. "That Ora Lee!" Mamaw would say. "She could get into more scrapes. Ran smack off the edge of the barn roof once, Floyd down on all fours chasing her. Knocked her out cold." "Billie was too much behind us to remember how crazy she was." "Oh, I remember," Billie would insist. "I was always about halfway scared of her." And she would give Lori a wink.

Aunt Billie never seemed to worry and fret over things. She was just happy and easy. She and Garth would be there on Sunday evenings sometimes. They would sit out in the backyard and finish off the last of the lemon meringue pie and make jokes. Lori would watch how her dad looked at them, with a kind of sad half-grin. And when they said good night and went off toward their junky old car they would hold hands and swing their arms, like kids.

Edna Earle didn't approve of Garth. "That ball-player husband of hers," she called him. And he really had been a professional baseball player at one time. He had played second base for the Shreveport Sports under the management of Salty Parker, and had been quite a star around the Texas League. But an inability to turn a fast double play without throwing the ball away had kept him out of the majors. After a severely pulled hamstring in his fifth season he had quit baseball and gone to work on the assembly line at the aircraft plant.

But Edna Earle did not approve of him. She would never let Lori accept Aunt Billie's invitations. There would come a phone call on a Thursday night near bedtime, say, and Aunt Billie would invite her to go to the Friday night baseball game. (The Fort Worth Cats, a farm club of the Dodgers.) But her mother would always have some reason why she couldn't go. "Another time, hon," Aunt Billie would say. Or she would call on a Saturday afternoon and ask if Lori would like to come over for supper and spend the night. Garth might be gone somewhere, and she would say they could have fun, just the two of them. "Please, Mama," she would beg, "can I?" "Certainly not. It's church night." Meaning the night before church the next morning—"Church Eve," she might have said. Meaning Billie might not get her home in time to get ready for Sunday school, which began at nine-thirty and was never missed. And after Lori hung up she would say, "That Billie. Never stops to think." And Lori would hope she would grow up to be just like her.

She did get to spend the night with Mamaw, though, at her linoleum-floored apartment on Hemphill. There was a high double bed in one room, with a dresser and a tall old wardrobe against one wall and two rocking chairs by the window. In the other room there was a kitchen stove in one corner, and a sink, and at the other end a

white-painted table at a deep window. Outside the window there was
a lattice with some kind of twining plant making a thick green screen
that filtered the sunlight. The bathroom was down the hall, shared
with two other apartments.

From the time Lori was six years old until she was lost in pubescence
and too grown up to spend the night with Mamaw, she went there
every Friday. They would have bacon and fried potatoes for supper,
or chicken and dumplings, maybe, and sometimes Mamaw would
have made a big batch of the wonderful plain cookies she called tea
cakes. Then they would listen to the ball game or play checkers or
dominoes—until Lori learned to beat her; then it was checkers or
nothing.

Lori never minded her pottering ways then. She thought they were
funny. Mamaw had all kinds of comical ways—her snuff dipping, her
refusal to look before stepping off a curb, her stockings down around
her ankles, her talkiness and funny expressions. When she spoke of
Uncle Floyd's years in the Navy or of one of Lori's cousins in the service, he was always "across the water"—she had no notion of
geography, one foreign country was the same as another. If you step
on a nail, she said, hang it over the door where you'll walk under it, so
your foot will heal faster. If you have a sore throat, take a swig of
kerosene. For chicken pox, take the child to the chicken yard early in
the morning, so the chickens will fly over coming off their roost, and
the sores will go away. Oh, she had dozens of them; she really believed them. When Lori had the chicken pox she was all upset because
Edna Earle and E. Z. did not have chickens. She went into a two-week
mad fit when Uncle Floyd said the chicken pox would only get covered
up with chicken shit anyway. How had he learned to talk like that!
And she could never get used to modern things. She called the tele-
vision set the telephone and said she had talked to Ora Lee on the
radio.

Later, when Lori was too old to spend the night at Mamaw's old
apartment with the chamber pot under the bed, it wasn't funny
anymore. She was so ignorant! So tacky! "Oh, now," said Aunt Billie.
"That's not the way to look at it."

She didn't know what to think anymore. She kept her nose in her
library books, hoping her mother wouldn't come along and notice the
dirty words, and mused through the picture box, and watched and
listened with greater interest.

III

TUESDAY, THE DAY BEFORE the Fourth of July picnic, Lori spent wandering in and out of the kitchen where her mother and grandmother were getting things ready for the big occasion. It was now being considered a full-fledged Family Reunion. Another letter had come from Ruth saying that they were driving up after all and might even get Elmo to come along. That meant they would all be together for the first time in . . . they couldn't remember when. So everything had suddenly gotten elaborate and organized. They were all going to meet at the park and everybody bring something. It was tacitly understood, though, that Edna Earle would bring the most. She always did, then always complained about it.

It was very hot, nearly a hundred and not a cloud in sight. "Oo-ee, if it's like this tomorrow, and us out in it all day!" Mamaw said. Edna Earle said they better hope it was. "If it rains, that whole bunch will come tromping in here. I can just see what a mess. But we could sure stand a little cooling off." Their backs and underarms were soaked, and they drank iced tea all afternoon and talked and talked. Reminiscing. Mamaw poured out a disconnected eulogy of the past. There would be a little space of silence and she would start up again, "Edna Earle, do you mind the time . . ." Over and over.

Lori listened. And to cover her listening, so that she would not seem excessively interested and thereby uncertain of her own generation's superiority and thus vulnerable, somehow, she made intermittent and ineffectual gestures of help. Mostly she got in the way. Edna Earle had never made her help around the house. "She'll have to do all that soon enough," she would explain sadly. And that was fine with Lori, except when Mamaw seemed to think that meant she wasn't any good. She wished Lori was more like a girl at her apartment, who, she said, was real smart. Smart? Lori knew her at school, and she barely passed her subjects. But she could get breakfast on weekends and clean house for her mother, and that made her smart. It wasn't fair.

So it was without the least enthusiasm—or skill, either—that she pitched in with her pretenses of help. She dried a few dishes, she shelled hard-boiled eggs and left them rough and ragged, she peeled potatoes and took away chunks of white flesh while leaving patches of brown. Luckily, they didn't notice. Working, talking, they occupied a world compounded of domesticity and memory, from which she was virtually shut out. Her mother frosted a cake. Mamaw, stooped and half blind, bent over a mixing bowl, dabbling with her fingertips in the unmeasured mess of flour and shortening that would be piecrusts. Her knobbed old fingers, bony but hung with folds of silky loose skin, worked in and out, gathering and melding the dough, and every minute or two she lifted the bowl up to her better eye to see if it was right yet.

Lori wondered, had Mama sat in the kitchen and watched Mamaw like this when she was a girl? Had Mamaw watched her own mother and even grandmother? For she must have had one, though Lori had never heard about her. Maybe this was the regressive linkage of the chain of foremothers, this kitchen-sharing, kitchen-lore, a parallel to the history-book linkage of the forefathers. The succeeding links in the chain were added when they took up their own burden of child-work and kitchen-work. Miserably, she hacked out a potato eye. It was either do this, which she hated and had no knack for, or remain cut off, excluded. And it wasn't even that this chain, the only one available to her, was so paltry a parallel to the chain of the forefathers. In a way, it didn't even exist; it hadn't been worth keeping pieced together. "My grandfather came from Tennessee," Mamaw would say. "He was a good farmer and a good blacksmith. His daddy had come over from somewhere across the water." But when Lori asked her about her grandmother or the women before, there was only a blank. They had died, or she couldn't remember; it didn't matter. And of her own mother, Lori's great-grandmother Guthrie, she could only say, "My daddy said she had red hair and the narrowest waist. I took over the cooking and washing when she died."

"Edna Earle, you mind the time we went to Homecoming?"

"Oh yes, certainly, the only Homecoming we ever went to since Lori's been old enough to remember, I guess."

That was the trip when she was nine. She remembered it, all right!

"That was the time Janey's mother had the heart failure and E. Z. slept through the whole thing in Ruth's back room."

"Yes, I reckon it was. She sure could make watermelon rind preserves. You mind, she was just pouring up a jar of 'em in a cut-glass dish to take out to the table when she fell over."

Lori hadn't known about that. Apparently death was one of those subjects they kept from the young.

"Mm-hm." Edna Earle was finishing up the frosting on the cake, turning her knife to make little peaks all over the top, and she didn't pay much attention.

"Course, the Byerses always had the best melons. Old man Byers did before we moved away."

"Are those pies about ready for the oven? You better sit down for a while."

Mamaw wiped her hands on her apron, sat down beside the table, and pulled her lower lip, her eyes far off. After a few minutes she said, "Homecoming always called to mind so much graveyard-cleaning day."

"Same kind of spread," Edna Earle agreed.

"Lori, we used to have the best time then, late in the summer when they wasn't much to do but wait for the cotton to get ready to pick, everybody gather in families and bring food, big jars of sugar water—"

"Of what?" she asked, but there was no deflecting Mamaw from her stream of reverie for a mere explanation.

"—and clean the graves, cut down the weeds all around, then spread dinner. It was real nice." She went on and on about this family and that family that used to come to graveyard cleaning.

Lori examined her ragged fingernails minutely, wishing they were long and oval. What funny names all those people had! Epps, Ott, Barham, Noack, Fogle, McCash. She tried to imagine Mamaw among them, straight and muscular and stern-looking, like the picture, like a pioneer in a history book. She had done so much in her long life— picked cotton and chosen the best melon to cool in well water and killed snakes and put out fires. How had she been strong enough and how had she known enough to do it all? But now she was only stooped, wrinkled, and slovenly, with snuff running down her chin in little brown streams. So nearly illiterate she could barely spell through the newspaper and a Bible chapter a day.

"I don't guess nobody's keepin' up the graveyard nowdays. I don't guess we could even find your daddy's grave if we tried, Edna Earle, that's the truth."

"No, I guess not, Mamma. You know there wasn't any way I could help it."

"No. Nobody could. Nothin' would do for Buford but we had to sell off the place and come here and nobody left to keep care of things, after all that with Elmo."

"Ruth could have."

"Well, she couldn't hardly, with little ones to look after. And she had such a hard time with Virgie and all. We like to lost her right then. Them was bad times, the Depression and all."

"Well, she could've done something about Papa's grave, it seems like. It was too late when Elmo got out."

"Got out from where?" Lori had never heard about this.

"No cause for you to worry your head about that, honey." She put her right hand across her brow and leaned her head down on it, cupping the elbow in her left palm as she always did when she was troubled about something.

Edna Earle was chopping onions for the potato salad, with tears running down her face, and didn't notice. "He keeps up Jake Glover's grave," she said, with an edge to her voice that made Lori quit biting her cuticle and look up.

"Who's that?" she asked. "I never heard you talk about him before. He's not in the picture box, is he?"

"Oh, honey," Mamaw said, "you always want to know about everthing."

"Well, who was he?"

"Oh, Lori, that was your Aunt Billie's papa. You knew our papa died before she was born."

"Oh. Well, what ever happened to him? Why does Uncle Elmo keep up his grave?"

The old woman went out toward the bathroom with her mouth pursed up tight in the peculiar way she had when she was put out. She stumbled a little and caught herself against the door frame.

Her mother hissed at her in a loud whisper, "You and your inquisitiveness! I'll tell you this, and then you keep your mouth shut and quit upsetting your grandmother. She didn't know it when she married him, but he was a crazy man, really crazy. He was escaped from the asylum at Terrell and already married. Already married twice, even. They come and got him before Billie was ever born and the judge annulled the marriage and certified Billie a McCall and that's all there is to it. Now go on outside."

"But why does Uncle Elmo keep up his grave?"

"He has his reasons. Now you go on."

She got a library book and went to sit under the sycamore tree in front, where she could watch for John Pollard, a boy she knew at school who sometimes rode by on his bicycle and stopped to talk. John wasn't so great, but he was the closest thing she had to a boyfriend (though the son of the educational director at church had once kissed her behind the mimeograph machine) and that was reason enough to keep watch for him. She pretended to read, but her mind ran from her book to John Pollard to tomorrow's picnic to what they had been saying in the kitchen. Mamaw married to a crazy man, and then no marriage at all! She mused over that irruption of luridness into the long-familiar vista of the family past. As usual, whenever they approached anything important, anything that made a difference, they backed off into secrecy.

Her childhood had been filled with dialogues like today's. Every childhood disease had brought Mamaw by the first Hemphill bus to rub her aching legs till her poor hands were red and sore, or to lay a wrung-out washrag across her forehead. And while she nursed, she talked about their life down home. Fever was a droning strung across a background of pre-Depression East Texas. And mostly she had not cared, then, to listen. So what about all that? It was dead and gone. But now, grown to five feet eight, lanky as Mamaw must once have been, she was clumsy and aching for that popularity that she couldn't seem to achieve and that her mother wanted so badly for her. Struggling for a place among glittering girl compatriots with twice her "personality," and the faceless boys who pursued them, she had begun to brood over those overheard dialogues. She pondered each new discovery like a clue to a mystery, a partial enlightenment. She looked for the relevance of it all to herself. Sometimes she thought how different she was from Mamaw, sometimes how much alike. She projected herself far into an independent and vaguely professional future and imagined occasions of lavish and condescending generosity to a Mamaw miraculously rendered not only clean, stylish, and polite, but even grammatical.

It was hot under the sycamore tree, with no breeze to stir its big, pale leaves and the sun leaking through. She had no focus; her mind languished between these aimless musings and the story in her library book. She had sat there long enough to be half asleep when, after all,

John did ride by, turn, and come back, and her vigil was repaid with two minutes of halting conversation.

How was one supposed to talk to boys? There was no way to guess what they were thinking, what they would find interesting. At school she handled the problem by pretending to be engrossed in her books, but she was beginning to be afraid that something was wrong with her. She had decided that the first sign of her problem had been, long ago, her decision to run away when a fat boy named Curtis came over one Saturday morning when they were in the third grade. She still remembered having assumed he would chase her, as the boys and girls played chase on the school ground at recess, squealing and darting in their wild daily game in which she joined at the fraying edge of the group, never in its swirling center. So when she saw him coming, she ran. Curtis left. Yes, it was a bad beginning.

So the effort of talking to John when he stopped and stood looking at her over his silver handlebars made her dry-throated and dizzy. He would think she was stupid, a square. She mentioned the picnic. (A family picnic! Why should he care?) Talk flagged and then ceased utterly. John tossed his hair back with a jerk of the head and shoved off from the curb.

But she had despaired too soon. Something in her mumbled account of tomorrow's picnic and the family and Mamaw's harsh life had caught his attention. He circled back and stopped by the curb again. "My grandmother lives in Kinnedale," he said. "She's a real nice old lady. We go out there on Sundays a lot. Maybe you could go with us sometime."

Lori nodded, and again he rode off. How unexpected a success! She was plucked up from black despondency to the dizzy peaks of social success, of confidence in her female allure. She looked down at her undertanned legs below their cuffed shorts, nerved now to an appraisal of their shape and tone. The appraisal was not entirely gratifying, but at least she wasn't fat like her friend Elaine.

Maybe tomorrow Duane and Randy, Aunt Ruth's boys, would also look at her as if they thought she was good-looking. They were bound to like a city girl like herself. And even if they were cousins, they were the right age and the right sex to be interesting. Probably they were nicer now than they had been that other time, when she was nine. They had been about twelve and eleven then, a bad age for boys. Flushed with a new and altogether pleasant fantasy-sense of her appeal, she went in to see about something to wear to the picnic.

Mama and Mamaw were still in the kitchen. Mama was cutting up chickens, getting them ready to fry in the morning. "You know I could do that and save you the trouble," Mamaw was saying. She always wanted to wash the dishes or dust the furniture or do something that Edna Earle wouldn't let her do because she had cataracts and was never able to do a good enough job. Instead, Edna Earle told her it was about time to check on the pies, so she looked at them and then sat down in a kitchen chair and took her glasses off. Without glasses, her pale old eyes looked small and watery.

When Lori passed, she caught her hand and held it. "It's just bad to get old and no good for anything," she said.

Lori wanted to make the needed gesture of love. In natural contradiction of her desire to be appealing, alluring, sexy, she wanted still to be the child who spent the night with Mamaw and loved her simply. She remembered how Mamaw would get up in the middle of the night to make her a snack when she woke up from a dream and felt hungry, doing it gladly but scolding just enough to keep up appearances. But now she had grown to fourteen years old, a different person; she couldn't make those gestures. She felt everyone watching her, expecting goodness and niceness, freezing her up. She noticed things that she had been able to ignore then, and couldn't get past them: the bad grammar and country speech, the bagging hose, the bad stale smell that might have been either the natural smell of old age or Mamaw's own personal blend of snuff and false teeth and leaked urine.

So she was repelled by Mamaw's old-woman touch, and drew her hand away, and then felt ashamed of doing it. But Mamaw didn't notice. She was off again, away in the past, and chuckling to herself. What a fighter Floyd was back then, what quantities of food she had cooked, what healthy children she had had, how well-favored.

Edna Earle demurred. "I don't see how you can say that. Just little runts. All of us is undergrown, all but Ruth and Billie, I guess. I always did want to be tall, but what chance did we have? No medical care at all."

"Now don't start on that again. We had doctors if we needed 'em. People was just healthier then. We never heard of some of these things they have around here, asthmar and polio."

"We just never heard, that's all. Those woods was full of stunted, crooked people with about half a mind. Not that I have a whole one myself, but what wonder is it when I never had a chance for an education?"

"Oh—education! Education ain't everthing."

"No, it's not, but it's sure hard to get anywhere in the world without it. Lori," she said, turning suddenly on her where she loitered at the door, "can you imagine? Going with all the grades up through seventh in one room, and one teacher to do it all. Now what chance did we have? You just ought to be thankful you're where you are, I can tell you. Who was that you were talking to while ago? Not that boy from the grocery store, I hope. You need to make more friends."

She gaped, caught off guard again by one of her mother's quick shifts.

Mamaw shook her head. "Times was pretty hard when we first come here, though. I was just studyin' on that the other day. You know, with you and Floyd and Ora Lee all workin', and Cleora takin' in sewing off and on, and even renting in with Buford's family, they was times we nearly didn't make it. Yes, sir, hard times, for a fact."

"Now who was Buford, Mamaw?" After dawdling in the doorway, Lori sat down to listen again, and her mother brought her a Coke over ice.

"My brother, honey. My oldest brother was Charlie, he went out west in the oil field around Borger, then there was Buford. It was his doing that we had to sell the home place and move out here. Can't you remember him?"

"My word, Mamma, she was only four when he *died*. That's a long time ago." She put the cut-up chicken in the refrigerator and started to stir up cornbread to go with the black-eyed peas simmering on the back burner for dinner. "That's one thing I can say, though, we always had plenty to eat in the country. And it was the best food! Lots of fresh vegetables. That's the only thing kept us healthy, I guess. And food always tasted so much better cooked on the wood stove. Don't you think so, Mamma?"

"Oh, lands yes. No sir, my babies was never short of food, I can say that. I've seen the day I thought I was too tired to set one foot in front of the other, but it was out . . ."

They were off on that again. Lori took her Coke out to the back door to watch for her dad. He was due in for the holiday.

Leaves on the bushes in the backyard hung still and parched. The sky was like hot metal, hard and colorless. She stood with her back to them, waiting and watching, listening.

"The more I study on it," Mamaw began again, "the more I feel like it was that first baby not livin' that kept Floyd from bein' any account and Janey such a whiny do-nothin'. You know I don't generally talk against my own, now." It was true, she didn't. Lori listened. "But I been studyin' on this for quite a while now, and I think that's it, and we ought to remember and keep our patience. Our good Lord told us about throwin' the first stone, and I think that's what we all need to remember with Floyd and Janey. How would any of the rest turned out with a firstborn borned already turned blue and never breathed a breath and just as pretty and perfect a baby as could ever be, and so young. So I try to remember that when he calls me on the phone these nights."

"What do you mean, calls you? You didn't tell me about that."

"Oh, well, I don't have to tell you everthing. Like he used to, you know. In a condition."

"Well, I'll put a stop to that." Then in a minute, a little less sharply, "Does he cry?"

"Now, Edna Earle, that's my own boy. I never had any business sayin' a thing about it."

She banged the cabinet doors and pans for a while in a temper, heated a kettle of water and shucked corn. "What could be keeping him!" she complained. "I would like to get out of this kitchen some time before night."

But Mamaw had already shied off from the present, and her mind was running again on the time before, on the home place. "It was pretty bad for a fact, not havin' doctors anywhere close. You know I never held with you runnin' Lori to that doctor ever time she sniffled, but you're right about us bein' without doctors. It was bad. When I think of the suffering and the fright, and how long it took to go get the doctor, like that time Floyd like to cut his foot off."

Out on the porch, Lori winced but kept herself quiet. Cut his foot off—ugh!

"And you know I always will think that affected Ora Lee's mind, that time Floyd chased her off the barn roof and she was knocked out cold for so long. No doctor we could get quick. And ever one of my babies was nearly born before the doctor ever got there. Just hurt and hurt till you thought you couldn't hurt any more, and then hurt some more and pull on the bedpost . . ."

"Oh, well, Mamma, you don't need to go into all that."

"I mind one time, with Cleora I think it was or maybe it was Elmo, when old Doc Brewster come in the door, that Miz, oh, what was her name, Mizriz Something from over by the Otts, was just tryin' to break my water with a straight pin and—"

"Mamma, for heaven sake!"

"Oh yes, Lori's right out there. Well, I don't have no mind anymore." She sighed heavily.

Edna Earle raised her voice. "Anyway, Miss Lori, if you're listening out there, you can believe you ought to be thankful to be here with all the advantages, instead of down there like we was and having to do for ourselves or go without. Mostly go without."

Under her breath, Lori commented that at least she could talk in good grammar. She hated being told how thankful she ought to be. Her mother was always telling her that, and Mamaw always said it might be good for her to do without a little and do for herself like her own young-uns had to, and between them they froze her life into the shape of a moral lesson. She thought, if Aunt Billie were here she would laugh at them both and say not to listen to them. She and Aunt Billie would whisper about them and giggle, and it would be all right.

But she had heard a lot that day. There was now a mystery surrounding Uncle Elmo, and Uncle Floyd was a drinker—for even she knew enough to know that was the "condition" Mamaw referred to. She was impatient now for the picnic the next day, so she could watch and listen and maybe find out some more about these things. She wondered if her cousins, Duane and Randy, really would be there, and if they would have improved with time.

IV

IT WAS A GOOD DAY FOR A PICNIC, if you liked hot weather. The drooping trees and parched grass of the park were swathed in a haze of dust and heat shimmers. Even the whistle of the park train sounded worn out. Children ran around with flushed faces or sprawled on the ground; babies cried; fathers swore. But even though the back of Lori's dress was already soaked through when she climbed out of the car and her hair was stuck to her forehead in strings, she was all anticipation.

Billie had come over early that morning to help get ready. She and Edna Earle had fried the chicken and packed and repacked pickles and potato salad and sugar pies, while Lori lay on her stomach on the cool kitchen tile and read. About ten, when she was beginning to feel tired of reading and impatient to get going, Aunt Billie went past, red-faced and glowing from the heat and the hurry, and said that everything was ready and she was going to change clothes so they could go.

Edna Earle had expected Billie to come back in something a little dressier than denim shorts and a starched cotton blouse. She frowned just the least bit and asked if she had forgotten her makeup. But to Lori, Aunt Billie looked perfect. Her red hair was parted down the middle and pulled into two ponytails in rubber bands behind her ears. They gave her an easy, bouncy look and at once made Lori feel too dressed up, too "fixed."

When they got to the park, no one else had come yet except E. Z. and Garth, who had driven over early to hold a place. Partway down the bluff toward the Trinity River, where there was shade, they had pulled three tables end to end, with benches all along, and had claimed another table a few yards off to spread the food on.

Lori helped carry down the covered dishes and pans and the ice chest with the potato salad. Garth was off at one side throwing a baseball straight up into the air and catching it in his old glove. When they passed him he said, "How ya doin', Stilts," and neatly caught a high one. E. Z. got up from the bench where he had been lying and reading with his book propped on his chest, and went up to help carry. Then he stuck his book under his arm and sauntered off in the

direction of the tropical bird house. He would have no more to do
with this than he had to.

E. Z., having no family of his own, had once told Lori that one
small reason why he had married her mother—"the main reason, of
course, being my great infatuation with her obvious charms," he had
said, in his odd and unsettling way—was that she had a large and
cohesive family. "Cohesive and loving," he had told her, "that's what
I thought, and none of your city people, either, but actually from the
country, the rural South hallowed by Jefferson and Lee and Davis and
all those other great names. I was putting myself in touch with all that
tradition and stability and the simple people's simple tastes. Yes, sir,
that's what I thought." It was about the most words she had ever
heard him say at once, and at the time she could not formulate precisely what he meant by it, but she could feel its cutting edge. She knew
now, though, that he had been making an oblique protest against her
mother's concern with buying and keeping and taking-care-of, ac-
tivities in which she excelled, and maybe even hinting that he hoped
Lori would excel in something else. She knew, too, that her aunts and
uncles had caused him expense and trouble at various times. And she
could see for herself that they were not a cohesive and loving bunch.
But just for today it would be nice to pretend they were, and now here
he was, at the very time when things ought to be right, being morose
again, going off to the tropical bird house when Lori knew he didn't
care a thing about birds. No wonder people like Uncle Floyd thought
he was an oddball.

For quite a while no one else came. Edna Earle arranged and re-
arranged what she had brought, and fretted and said she hoped Ruth
and Jess hadn't run into any trouble. It was nearly twelve-thirty when
Aunt Cleora and Uncle Albert Barnes came down the slope. Though
the Reverend Barnes had phlebitis and limped slightly, he had parked
a good way off in order, he announced, that the others wouldn't have
so far to walk. He told them all several times that the walk did not
bother his leg significantly, smiling very broadly all the while and
wiping his head with a handkerchief.

It was clear from the start that Cleora was going to be difficult. She
brushed past Billie and led Edna Earle aside a few steps. Lori, watching
Garth throw the baseball high and catch it plummeting, could
overhear snatches of what they were talking about—Ora Lee and her
"flightiness" and her failure to "take any account of her respon-

sibilities." Aunt Cleora bobbed her slick red head in time to her stresses, then pursed her lips for one last look that said plainly, whatever happened wasn't her fault. When they came back she tried to pass it off, joking in her little bird voice that she was a "talky old woman." And while she went on chirping, Lori looked up and saw Jess, Aunt Ruth's scrawny husband, stretching and yawning beside their green Plymouth and her two cousins piling out and going at each other like scrappy puppies. Aunt Ruth swept down the weedy slope with her handbag flopping on her arm, uttering little glad cries in something like baby talk, and hugged everybody except Albert Barnes, with whom she shook hands. With that out of the way, she got down to business: Why wasn't Mamma here? Was she all right? Was Ora Lee coming? Where was Floyd? Where was E. Z.?

Meanwhile, Jess had come down grinning, showing his yellowed, inward-slanting teeth and fumbling with his hat. He, too, shook hands respectfully with the Reverend Barnes when the Reverend offered, and nodded and grinned all around. He told Lori to get up there and let them big strapping boys look her over. When he went to greet Garth, they called each other Old Pro and Old Cuss, and hit each others' shoulders lightly with fists before shaking hands.

Duane and Randy had started down with a cake and a big jug. They had shoulders now and great shocks of sandy hair, and shifting brown eyes that they narrowed at Lori appraisingly. But they only mumbled in her direction and went over to join their dad and Garth.

Garth was always a center of attention at family gatherings; naturally so, since he had been, in a small way, a celebrity. His baseball career was now long in the past, of course, but whenever he had an audience he enjoyed himself immensely. Now he backed off and started throwing to Duane and Randy. They shook their hands from the sting of the fast ones, and grinned.

Lori couldn't just stand around and admire them; it was embarrassing. So she walked up to their car to see if there was anything else to bring down, and there was Uncle Elmo, sitting in the backseat with his hands on his knees. He looked at her solemnly out of pale, expressionless eyes and said, "You're Edna Earle's girl, aren't you?"

They walked down together. He wasn't an old man, just a year older than her mother, but he moved and spoke like one. Lori wondered if he had been asleep in the car and wasn't fully awake yet. Then she realized he simply didn't know how to make conversation.

He stood a little back from the group swarming about the food table until Edna Earle looked up. Then he said, "Hello, Little Sister," and suffered himself to be hugged by Cleora before going to sit on a stump and watch the ball playing.

His smallness and passiveness, his general lack of anything remarkable, exasperated Lori. This was the uncle who generated the only real mystery of the family, and what mystery was there after all? Only an undersized middle-aged man, homely and countrified as could be because he hadn't had the nerve to get out of those pine woods and cotton fields and go to the city with the rest. No wonder they called him poor Elmo!

Then Uncle Floyd and his wife arrived with their two kids, Lori's cousins who went to North Side High, and Mamaw, who lurched stiff-legged down the hill carrying a department-store shirt box in her arms. She was all happiness, all wet eyes and wide smiles, but sucking up her lower lip to hide the gap where she had broken out a tooth from her plate. "Well, I swan," she said, "here you all are, ain't this the best thing, but where's Ora Lee?"

She hugged them all in turn and opened the shirt box for them to see. It was brimful of tea cakes, everybody's favorite. But when Edna Earle and Cleora started telling her she didn't have any business standing in the kitchen to do something like that (unlike Billie, who had said, "Oh, Mamma, how good!" and grabbed one right off) she got mad and reminded them that she had been cooking and washing before any of them were even thought of.

"I get so tired of you telling me all the time I can't do this, can't do that," she complained. She sat down abruptly and began to fan with an oval funeral-parlor fan she had pulled out of her purse, and fretted because Ora Lee hadn't come, worrying her free hand up and down on her knee.

They hung over her and clucked and said "Now, Mamma, don't fret," until Lori couldn't stand it and turned away. There sat Uncle Elmo, watching. "That makes me sick!" she told him. "They treat her like a baby!" She wished Mamaw would rise up and smite them, just tell them all to leave her alone. But of course she didn't. She just sat there looking weak and old and soaking it up.

For a while Lori joined the ball players gathered around Garth, and went through the motions of participating in a game of flies and grounders. But she knew that if the ball came toward her she would flinch and miss it. She was never any good at sports, only at spectator sports. But it was fun to get out there and fake it. Uncle Floyd went charging after the ball with a cigar in his teeth. Duane and Randy bumped into each other and rolled on the dusty grass whenever one came their way. Old Jess, who had booted the only one he had a chance at, clapped them shyly on the back any time one of them made a catch. E. Z. came back and went over to where Elmo sat watching the game, to shake hands and say hello.

About the time everything was all set and the ball game broken up and they were all about to make a surge at the food table, here came Ora Lee and Marvin Elkins, each with a round watermelon, and their stringy-haired little girl running ahead of them. Aunt Cleora, set on being snippy, pointed out that they hadn't planned on melon and probably didn't have enough paper plates, but Floyd said oh, hell, everybody would love a real Parker County melon and they could just set it out on newspaper later on. So they all filled their plates and found places at the table, all but E. Z. and Elmo, who sat apart on stumps and watched. Then there were seconds and for some of them, thirds, and for a while everyone was too stuffed and euphoric to move.

All together now, old antagonisms forgotten for a while, they relaxed and lingered at the table. Shade from the big cottonwood and pecan trees spread and merged and moved, and once everyone stood up to pull the tables over a few feet so the end where Mamma sat wouldn't be in the sun. Even E. Z. and Elmo finally moved in closer to listen to the reminiscing that began when somebody asked what grade all the young ones would be in this year, and went back from there to the one-room school back home and the girls in their long, brightly colored flour-sack bloomers and the fight Floyd and Elmo had with the Ott boys and the licking they got for it from the county superintendent. And then Edna Earle: "If we'd had a decent school some of us might have amounted to something," and Ruth: "If Floyd had got a licking for every fight he was in he never woulda growed up at all, instead of only growing halfway up." And Mamma, Mamaw, the old matriarch who didn't rule anymore, laughed and rubbed her eyes. Fall shopping and shoes and watching the money so close and the screaming fit Sis had in Clarksville that time, that last year, because Mamma wasn't going to buy her a new coat. And Ora Lee: "It wasn't really a *screaming* fit," and Floyd: "The hell it wasn't," and Mamma: "Floyd, I never brung you up to talk thataway." But she said it indulgently, as befits a favorite.

Then Elmo spoke, for the first time, to everyone or in effect to no one: "Yes, that was the year of the broken windows, that started all the trouble, and it never quit till we was all broke up." Lori stared. How could a few broken windows do all that? But they were in no mood to dredge up the somber things. They went around it like a stream around a rock, evaded that specter and moved their recollections further back to childhood, a time if not perfect then at least susceptible to being perfected in retelling. Their talk flowed through games and pets and the scrapes they had gotten into, stories in which they moved like innocent imps through a Huck Finn world as simplified, as far removed from present difficulties, as *The Three Bears* was from the smutty jokes whispered in high school hallways. Floyd poked Ora Lee in the ribs and said that you could write a book out of all the crazy things she had done when she was a kid, and somebody ought to. And they all laughed at that and added their own favorite Ora Lee stories. It made Lori wish she had brothers and sisters with whom she could accumulate a body of shared lore.

But then Cleora said distinctly, "It was running off from home with that boy that was the craziest stunt."

She shouldn't have broken the family taboo. Everyone fell silent and looked uneasy; in the sudden quiet Lori could hear the whistle of the park train. Marvin Elkins stood up and went off without a word toward his car. Only Mamma, Mamaw, still the matriarch when she could gather herself, cleared her throat and confronted the breach: "Cleora, I don't know as that was rightly necessary."

Cleora asserted the right and wrong of it by her silence and her rigid posture, while Ora Lee glared across at her. Billie looked around in desperation for some way to smooth things over, and when her eye lit on the box of tea cakes she asked if somebody besides herself wouldn't like one to finish off with. So the box was passed around.

E. Z. stood up and yawned. "Well, I know those were fun times, living off the fat of the land and all," he said dryly, "but I'm just roasting here. Are we going to cut those watermelons later on?" He retrieved his book from the stump where he had been sitting, and went off again.

Then there was a general breaking up and stirring around. They started clearing away, and Floyd and Garth and Jess said they'd better go look for Marvin Elkins. Mamma turned her favorite chair away from the table and sat bent and brooding. Lori, ignoring for once her mother's scowls of disapproval, rambled off to the zoo with Duane and Randy.

Past the park train station and the other rides, where the path was deep in warm sand, past the aquarium and the tropical bird house. They went up and down the hot sidewalks, looking at antelopes, elephants, bears. A ragged gray wolf trotted listlessly up and down a cage like a corridor, his tongue hanging out, as trapped in his eternal present as the family were trapped in their past. Flies clustered over a pile at the near end of the cage. Lori felt embarrassed by the conspicuous excrement, embarrassed by the smell everywhere and by the monkeys playing with their red members and by the swing of the lion's testicles as he paced his cage.

Against the background of the hot zoo stink she could smell the sour uric odor of the boys' underarms when they bumped against her as they walked. Duane took off his shirt, and the two puckered brown circles on his slick chest drew her eyes. She was uncomfortable, but at the same time she felt expanded and daring, and tried to act as though she had not spent all her adolescent days in a quiet frame house, reading and daydreaming and chafing under her mother's superintendence.

The boys loitered along, unmoved by the exhibit but flicking their eyes at all the kids that passed and poking each other with their elbows. Lori couldn't think of anything to say. They seemed to be looking at her on the sly, and they talked to each other in a kind of code that she couldn't penetrate. After a while they sat on a bench and drank Cokes, and the boys asked about her school, the kids she knew and what kinds of things they did, all sorts of things. They mentioned that they were both on the football team at their school, and she realized that she was expected to show admiration.

Finishing his Coke, Randy put his fist to his chest and belched, then, abruptly polite, suggested that she come for a visit sometime.

What a nice idea! Why had she once thought they were so awful? She said she would ask her mother. That is, if Aunt Ruth wanted her to come.

"Yeah, you do that. We got some friends you could meet, maybe have a nice time. Ain't that right, Duane?"

"Oh, yeah. She'd like ol' Jerry, don't you reckon?"

"Sure she would."

With that, Duane and Randy seemed to have had enough of the zoo. They stood up, Duane put his shirt back on, and she trailed after them along the baking sidewalks back to the picnic area.

Except for the ones who had gone after Marvin, they were all still gathered together and still, of course, talking about old times and the home place—where this or that grew, what the cotton sold for, how hard it had been when they first came to Fort Worth, whether it was really smallpox they had that time or only chicken pox, as the doctor who quarantined them said. Now, though, they talked low and unsmiling. "Depression . . . trouble . . . sold . . ." "It was so hard, so hard, goin' off and leavin' everything I knowed, and the family broke up . . ." "Mamma, now . . ." "Do you think you would have left if there hadn't been so much trouble?" Ora Lee asked. "Maybe if I hadn't done my crazy thing." "Oh, honey, yes, we woulda gone, we'd a-had to, with the Depression, and Buford after me like he was. I didn't know where to turn."

"Well, I never have been sorry. Not once we got through that first year or two, anyway. What opportunity was there, off down in the country? Tacky little house, work all the time . . ."

"Oh, now, Edna Earle. We was a sight better off than here, before the Depression we was, anyway."

The lament went on: Depression, taxes, split up, dead. Then: oil. Oil wells coming in a straight line from Talco right toward the home place, and they still had mineral rights on it.

Elmo sat apart, pulling his lip—Mamaw's gesture. Lori went over and sat on the ground beside him. What were they talking about? Wouldn't he explain some of it? Her mother and Mamaw never really told her about things, but just talked to each other so that she couldn't get at things and really understand.

"Why do you want to know?" he asked.

"I don't know, I just do."

She could see him turning it over in his mind before saying, more to himself than to her, "Things never was the same after the Depression started and then all the trouble. It all went bad. Sometimes I wish I never had growed up to that time, or time had stopped about 1928, with Mamma like she was then, and Edna Earle like she was, and the others."

"But what happened?"

"You ought to know. You're growing up now, and it's fair that you ought. I don't know, there's never any time . . ."

A car stopped, squealing, and doors slammed. The men—Floyd, Garth, Jess—came down the slope, grinning and pleased with themselves. Marvin Elkins followed, carrying his guitar.

Floyd swaggered up to Ora Lee and kissed her cheek. "We brung you back your man, Sis," he said. "Maybe you should tell your redheaded sister there to mind her tongue a little better."

Mamaw pulled him down and sniffed. "Floyd McCall, you been drinkin' beer. I can smell it all over you."

But he smacked her on the cheek, too, and told her she shouldn't let that bother her. "Good beer never hurt any man. Right, Marvin?"

Marvin could only shy off from Ora Lee's glare, but Garth and Jess said that was right, and Billie pulled Garth down to sit on the ground beside her, and tugged a twig of his hair.

Floyd announced that Marvin was going to play some before they cut the melons, and without a word, standing at the end of the table under a sycamore tree with leaves as big as fans, Marvin slipped the guitar strap over his neck, licked his lips, and began. He played for himself, it seemed, more than for anyone else, never looking at them at all but smiling a little and sometimes moving his lips slightly. He was a small man, with a perpetual black shadow of beard and black, beady eyes that had a kind of scared look except when he took up his guitar. He played a wonderful, hard-driving bluegrass that never rested till the end. Then, for the first time, he glanced up at them from under his heavy eyebrows, before playing another just as fast and full of runs. Next he played a medley of the old sentimental western songs that the Light Crust Doughboys used to play when he was with them, before Aunt Ora Lee made him quit. In a flat, thin voice he sang "Riding Down the Canyon" and "Cool, Clear Water" and the others. But it wasn't real, not like what had gone before. No one there had ever ridden down a canyon to watch the sun go down, and Lori began to feel faintly embarrassed. A group of kids from another picnic down the way who had drifted over to listen drifted away again and turned on a radio.

Still, it was fine, sitting there in the shade, listening, everyone easy and enjoying themselves. Everyone except Mamaw, who was still mad and pouting. Billie and Garth smiled at each other in a shared-secret sort of way, and Jess patted his foot. If Marvin Elkins could have kept playing for an hour or two everything might have been fine. But Edna Earle had never liked music, so she started cutting wedges of watermelon and passing them around, and Marvin put his guitar back in its case.

Everybody, taking a first bite, said what good melon, just ripe enough and not too ripe—just what you're supposed to say when a watermelon is good. But Mamaw wouldn't have any. She sat with her back turned, puffed up, as they said, like a puff adder. They shook their heads and giggled behind their hands. But Floyd, wound up now, wouldn't let her alone. He teased, clowned, mimicked. "Hellfire, Mamma," he said, "if that mouth of yours was drawed up any tighter, you wouldn't be able to squeeze a English pea through there. Not even a toothpick. Here, here's a toothpick, I'm going to see if I can."

Sitting off to the side, Lori could see a smile begin to twitch around her mouth. She could never resist Floyd, who knew that teasing was the way to get around her. And it would have worked this time, too, but Cleora ruined it.

She sprang at him and grabbed his arm, and told him to leave her Mamma alone. "You ought to be ashamed," she told him, "coming here and spoiling the day for the poor old thing, with your going off and drinking and language. And now making fun of her besides."

Edna Earle chimed in and told what she should have kept to herself, that Floyd had been calling Mamma when he was drinking and getting her upset. Then it really broke loose. Floyd yelled at them to shut up, damn it, and called Cleora a bossy old bitch. He said he was sick of them hovering over Mamma and telling her she was no good for anything anymore and had to be taken care of and bossed around. They acted like she was half dead already, he said. He threw in words that startled Lori, words she never heard at home, and told them to leave Mamma alone and she could take care of herself. She was tugging at his arm and saying, "Now hush, Floyd, now don't go gettin' mad." But they all ignored her, all but Billie, who looked as if she'd been hit in the face. She ran from one to the other, begging them to stop, to think about Mamma, but it was no good.

"Oh, yes, Floyd," Edna Earle hissed. "You would say let her alone, wouldn't you? That's just what you do, all right, is let her alone— never help with her bills, never see after her, just leave the whole burden on us."

E. Z. took hold of her elbow and told her to stay out of it, to let it alone, but she shook him off without even a look.

Cleora said yes, that's what she'd been telling Albert, that none of them did their fair share. She bobbed her head for emphasis. "You just put it on Edna Earle and me and forget about it," she said. "All of you do."

Ruth began to cry and said it wasn't her fault, she couldn't do any more than she did.

"Maybe not," Cleora conceded. "And Billie and Garth do a little. But the burden of her falls on Edna Earle and me, and it's not fair, that's all."

Mamma begged them to just let it go, she didn't want all this trouble. But it was no use. They were all going at each other, yelling and making accusations, all but Billie, who had turned to Garth's arm as a refuge, and Albert Barnes, who seemed intent on keeping up a look of dignity. "Come along, Cleora," he said. "There's no use staying here any longer." Elmo hopped around making helpless gestures. E. Z. shook his head and told Lori to help him start loading the car. But she couldn't leave it. It was appalling, and she would have liked to run away, but she had to see it out. She thought Mamaw looked as though something in her that had already crumbled was now being ground to powder. In the part of her that had been Mamaw's favorite, she wanted to go to her and speak the right reassuring word, but she could only sit still and watch.

When the furor of squabbling abated for a minute, Edna Earle, in a strained voice, urged them all to be reasonable. Couldn't they all just settle down and discuss this thing calmly? There were bills, after all, and Mamma's pension didn't much more than pay her rent, and they needed to know what to count on from everybody. "There are going to be big bills sooner or later," she said. "We all know that. Of course, for an emergency there's that little insurance policy that could be cashed in, but that's not much, and—"

"What insurance policy?" Wet-eyed, Mamma lifted her head from the cup of her palm.

"Oh, you know, Mamma. The policy you bought paid-up when you sold the home place."

"Why, you know that's gone."

They all looked at each other in surprise, except Floyd, who continued to pace the hard-packed dirt beside the picnic table. What did she mean, it was gone?

"Why, you know you all agreed to me cashing it in that time."

So then it came out that Floyd had told her they had all agreed for her to cash in the policy and give him the money, and in return he wouldn't get a share if they ever struck oil on the home place. It was years ago; she was sure they had put it all in writing. She stood and turned stiffly, shuffling her feet in the dust, to ask Elmo's corroboration. But he could only shake his head.

"I never signed no paper like that," he said. "I'm sorry, Mamma."

Lori could see by the way Floyd's face lost expression and his eyes flicked around at the others that this was a subject he had never expected to come up. They all stared at him, then all yelled at once, while Janey, his silent wife, started uncomfortably into the distance.

He yelled back at them that it didn't make any difference, they hadn't missed it, and when the money was needed he'd pay. "Don't you worry about that," he said. "I can pay when I need to." He glared around at them all and motioned to Janey to come on. Their two kids had already started toward the car, looking caught at something, sorry to have been caught, but glad to have done it.

Edna Earle yelled after him that he'd better stay and do some explaining. E. Z. told her again to let it go. He might have no illusions about his in-laws, but he at least wanted peace.

But she kept squalling at Floyd that he couldn't leave now. "Tell us this much, anyway. Have you cheated us out of the mineral rights on the place, too? At least we might be able to get that out of it, or have you stolen that, too?"

Floyd turned on her then and pointed his stubby finger at her and fairly spat out, "You shut up, you bitch."

At that Elmo went into a little crouch, and Lori thought he was actually going to spring on Floyd, but just at that moment Mamaw turned again and tottered forward a step, then fell back into her chair with her left hand fluttering between her face and her chest and her right clutching the arm of the chair. For a minute it was as if no one else was seeing and Lori couldn't make them see and do anything for her. Then, they gathered in, all hushed.

She lay back in the chair, gray and gasping, and stared blankly up at them. Ora Lee shrieked and squealed—hysterics had always been her strong point—while the rest lowered their voices and asked her terse, hesitating questions. "What is it—?" "Is it any better, Mamma—?" "You breathing easier now—?" "You with us, Mamma—?"

"You know where you are—?"

Billie slipped in under the others and knelt to loosen her dress, then fanned her with a folded grocery sack. They waited.

Crouched on the other side of her chair from Billie, Lori held Mamaw's hand tight and looked into her homely old face to see which way it was set. After a while E. Z. suggested they call an ambulance. But at that she made a few quick blinks, her tongue ran around her open mouth, and Lori felt her gathering herself to focus on that idea and deal with it.

"No ambulance," she said, very low first and then again, louder. "I don't need no ambulance nor no hospital." She drew her feet under herself and grasped the folded metal arms of the lawn chair, but remained where she was.

Billie asked if she was sure.

"Yes, I'm sure, plague take it. I musta got overheated, that's all. I'm ready to go if you all are."

She pulled herself up, shook off their hands, and started past the picnic table and up the slope. But she veered off target, away to the right, and fetched up against a scrub oak.

Then they knew that it was time for them to carry her.

V

THEY TOOK HER BACK to the house and got her to bed in Lori's room. Then everybody stood around while Edna Earle phoned for Dr. Kneeland and for Cleora. She set out odds and ends to snack on during the waiting.

They kept talking about the same things as back at the park—expenses, the mineral rights they had kept when the place was sold, the oil wells coming in a straight line from Talco. But now it was only talk. For the time, the rancor had been drained off.

It seemed like a long time before the doctor came. Lori kept going to the bedroom door and looking in at Mamaw. She seemed to be asleep. She lay with her long hands palms-together under her slack cheek, one bunioned foot sticking out from under the sheet.

Cleora arrived, wailing that it was all her fault because she had fussed with Floyd and got Mamma upset. She walked back and forth, clasping her hands and crying out loud until Floyd told her for God's sake to quit taking on so, Mamma wasn't dead yet.

The next time Lori went to look in at her, her eyes were open and fixed on the doorway. She beckoned Lori in and asked what everybody was doing. "Waiting for Dr. Kneeland," Lori said. She pulled the curtain back and looked out the front window. No sign of him yet.

"That was your mother's doin', I know. She always would run to the doctor ever excuse." She turned on her back and lifted her head, then sat up and leaned against the headboard of the bed. They had taken her dress off, leaving her in a white cotton slip with a narrow strip of eyelet embroidery around the top. It looked like a child's, with the gathered bust sections empty on her chest. "Oh, how many times I have been here with you sick in bed," she said, "right in this very bed. You always knew to call for your Mamaw."

"I know it, Mamaw."

"Now I'm callin' for you. Listen, come sit here by me a minute, I want to tell you something." She took Lori's hand in hers and patted it. "Such pretty hands, just as soft! You never had no work to toughen 'em up like I had when I was a girl, even before my mother died and I married your granddaddy."

Lori turned her head away. The same old story that she was so tired of!

"Now listen. Don't you let 'em take me to no hospital."

"What could I do, Mamaw? They wouldn't pay any attention to me. Anyway, you're not going to need it."

"You stick up for me, you hear? Don't let 'em forget. I don't want in no hospital."

Lori nodded. Might as well humor her. But it was so stupid, the way she was scared of hospitals. It didn't make sense.

She sat there for a long time, or it seemed like it. Mamaw kept tight hold of her hand, but slid back down in the bed and lay on her back, very still, unbothered by the little wad of hair pinned on the back of her head. Her mouth, hanging open, looked dirty, snuff stained, and her skin was a dingy yellow that lay in loose folds. There didn't appear to be anything particularly wrong with her, but she exhaled an odor of rot. Lori wished she could get away from it. She turned her head away.

After a while Aunt Billie came to the door and looked in. She lifted her eyebrows questioningly and laid her hands together beside her cheek, asking if Mamaw was asleep. Lori nodded, slid her hand away, and tiptoed out. At the door Billie pinched her and said she was sweet to sit with Mamaw, but didn't she want to go outside with the young ones? She didn't really, but when Aunt Billie said it, it seemed like the thing to do.

Outside, she could hear the sharp *bonks* of a neighbor family's croquet game. There was a nice glow from their strings of yard lights, and their voices drifted happily over the backyards. She felt shut out and blue.

She went down the driveway toward the front, thinking to find her cousins. Sure enough, they were all there, sitting on the porch. She stopped and listened. She had walked on the strip of thick Saint Augustine grass that ran beside the driveway, and they hadn't heard her coming. Uncle Floyd's daughter was finishing some awful story, and the others laughed, low and furtively. "I'd like to see you tell a joke like that to Lori," one of the boys said. "She wouldn't even know what it meant." "Yeah," said Floyd's boy, "she gives me a pain." "Yeah," said the girl, "she thinks she's such hot snot." "Oh, she ain't so bad."

"Not so bad": it wasn't much of a defense. She stood in the dark, and her breath came in narrow stabs. She clenched her fists; she *wouldn't* cry. As quietly as she could, she backed away and eased down the side of the house again, retreating. She felt very lonely and let down. It had not been a good day after all. She tried going in, but she couldn't find any place to herself. The doctor had come, and people were all over the house, it seemed, talking about what they would do if it was this and what they would do if it was that. So she went out again to try the back yard.

A voice from the darkness beyond the range of the floodlight startled her. When she stepped out of the light, she could make out Uncle Elmo, sitting alone in one of the rusted metal lawn chairs. She pulled up another, and for a while they just sat there. They heard the doctor leave, and they heard the croquet balls still going *bonk* across the back yards. Voices would surge through the open windows and recede. Lori thought of going to find out what Dr. Kneeland had said, but there didn't seem to be any use. They would find out soon enough.

Then the relatives were leaving, first Ora Lee, crying, with Marvin Elkins trailing after her, then Billie and Garth with arms around each other's waist. ("They act like newlyweds," Mama had said once, in disgust.) There were smatters of talk about who would spend the night where, but no one came to take Elmo away to bed. The headlights of all their cars flashed on against the garage and then swung toward the neighbor's back yard, as one after another, they backed and turned into the street. There was a sound of water in the kitchen sink and dishes clattering. E. Z. came to stand on the back steps, but if he knew they were there he decided against joining them.

They sat there in the dark and talked for a long time. Talk with Elmo was slow; there were a lot of silent spaces. Lori felt impatient, there was so much he could tell her, if he would; yet she managed not to show it. What had Mamaw been like, she asked, all those years ago? In the picture she looked like she could do everything, she looked like a real pioneer.

It was a good question to ask; it pleased him. He knew the picture she meant, he said. Pioneer was right. She had even lived in a log cabin when she first married his papa. Did Lori know that?

She shook her head. She was glad to find it out. It was a good thing to know. It fitted her old imaginings.

He fell quiet again for what seemed like several minutes, then cleared his throat and went on, with stops and pauses, as if picking carefully through his available stock of memories and words. "She was quite a woman, I'll tell you that, and she didn't have no easy time of it."

She was so tired of people telling her how hard they had it and how easy everything was for her! But she held her tongue.

He talked about how hard Mamma had to work, and how strong and able she was, and how neglectful they had all been of their duty to her, never helping out as they ought. She must have been somebody more than human, he said, to hold everything together like she did. But it never seemed to get too much for her until near the end, when Ora Lee went bad and that Jake Glover was hanging around and making trouble.

What trouble? she asked. What had happened? But he didn't notice. He had to tell it in his own way if he was going to tell it at all. She would learn more that night than she had ever learned before, but she was going to have to wait for it.

He started again. "I remember when I was just a little thing—not more'n five, I guess, because my daddy was there. I was settin' on the porch beside Mamma's chair in the evenin' and lookin' up at her while she combed out her hair for it to dry. It was real long and brownish red then, all around her head and down around her shoulders. And I looked up at her and thought what a beautiful mother and what a beautiful dress she had on—it all faded out and just a plain old work dress, probably; she never had much else, anyway not to wear on a Saturday night to set on the porch. And I thought how happy and safe I was, 'cause she'd always be right there and just that way. My daddy musta been sick then. He was in the bed right inside the window by us, I remember, and he said, 'Elmo, you got to take good care of your mama when you get big enough. I wasn't good enough for her and look what I'm lettin' her in for. She don't deserve this hard work, and you children mustn't let her down like I'm doin'.' Or somethin' like that. He knew then that he was dyin', I guess. I've always remembered that. We let her down, after all, but there wasn't nothin' could get the best of her."

It was like he wanted to stop there, but she couldn't let him. This was her chance. He had to tell her what he meant, what had gone wrong, what Jake Glover had done, what made them leave.

"Oh, the government, Lori, the Depression." She had heard that before. That couldn't be all of it. "Well, then Floyd bein' so restless and wantin' to go, and Mamma's brother here in Fort Worth, Buford, he was telling her to sell and go. Wanted to get hold of what little money she'd get for it, I guess. Then Ora Lee run off."

"What do you mean, run off?"

"Just run off. She was restless, like Floyd. They was always a lot alike, full of meanness, or full of fun, whichever. So, she went off with some boy, never married him. It like to killed Mamma. The one thing she had was knowin' she'd raised us right. She felt like she owed that to our daddy, I guess, and she couldn't let down the least bit for fear she'd do somethin' he wouldn't have if he'd lived. Especially after she married Jake Glover and it turned out so bad, I think she felt that way. She always kept everything unfitting out of the way, especially away from the girls. The animals and all, you know. And bad talk. Everything. And then Ora Lee goin' off in sin like that. It like to killed her."

"Going off in sin": it was a lurid, exciting thing to hear. It had a whorish ring. She imagined Aunt Ora Lee in scarlet and purple, and heavy makeup.

He sighed. "And then after Jake Glover burned the house down and they all left—"

"Burned the house down!" This was her very own family, and someone had burned their house down!

"Oh, not the one we was livin' in. A little old house on a back piece of the land, that we was goin' to move into so we could rent out the big one. It was more or less the place I live in now. Anyway, even after all that, and they all left, even then Mamma and Edna Earle mighta come back and then everything woulda been fine, and we coulda been happy, the three of us, but I had to spoil it all for good."

He talked in circles! "What do you mean, you spoiled it?"

"Oh, they didn't tell you that, either, huh? Well." He sat mulling over that surprise.

From the circle of light by the back door, E. Z. said she should come in now. But of course she couldn't stop to pay attention to him. She didn't even stop then to wonder how long he had been standing there. Now that she was this close, she had to press Elmo for the rest, even if he didn't want to say it. She demanded again, what was it that he had done?

"I shot Jake Glover," he said. "I killed him. He come into the store where I was workin', right there in Cut Hand, and I shot him square in the chest with a shotgun." He saw again the weasel face, the muddy overalls, Papa's shotgun under the counter. "It was with old man Badgett's shotgun," he said. "He kept it there for protection."

"Why? Why did you do it?"

E. Z. stepped out of the circle of light into the shadowless dark where they were sitting and said that she'd better go in. It was very quiet. The croquet game had stopped some time ago. There were only lightning bugs out now, blinking soundlessly off and on in the rear of the yard and the alley. "Go on in, Lori," he repeated.

She hesitated, looking from one to the other. "Why?" she asked again. "Why did you shoot him?"

"He said somethin'," he told her. "Somethin' he deserved to die for." A little piece of that ass, he had said. He was counting on getting a little piece of that. Edna Earle. "He said give him the money, what was in the register. He was going to rob the place. That's why Badgett kept the gun. So I done it. So wasn't it like I was the hand of the Lord in it?" He stood up and leaned over her, shoving his face into hers. "I was goin' to be a preacher. I was supposed to preach that very next Sunday. But instead I shot Jake Glover for somethin' he deserved to die for, and they sent me away to Huntsville."

Then she knew that was all she would get this time. It was enough, anyway, too much. She didn't want to hear any more, even if there was more. Her father and the strange lone uncle appeared to share a great fatigue that had dragged them both down into being older than their years. She turned away toward the floodlight. Her father thumped Elmo's shoulder once with the heel of his hand and asked if he was ready to turn in. No, not for a while yet. He hesitated, then turned away with her and went back to the house. They dashed past the floodlight where the June bugs zoomed and bumped, then, by shared impulse, paused on the screened-in porch.

She started to ask him if he had known that Uncle Elmo had killed a man and gone to prison, but then she realized that of course he had known, he had to have known. Instead, she asked, "Do you think that's really why he did it?"

He shrugged. "Who knows?"

"I still don't understand!"

"No, I don't expect you do," he said. "I've been trying for sixteen years to figure out this simple country family I married into, and I

haven't succeeded yet. But maybe you will. You're getting off to a
good start."

Still they stood. He asked if she'd had a good time today. She
shrugged. Had the boys been teasing her too much? "Oh . . ." She
wanted to tell him all of it and ask what they had meant by the things
they said, the way they acted. There had been those jokes on the front
porch. But she only said that she didn't think they talked very nice.
"Probably not," he said. "Don't let that bother you too much. But
I wouldn't mention it to your mother if I were you."

Of course, she would never have dreamed of that.

Edna Earle came into the kitchen then and saw them on the porch.
"There you are," she said. "What on earth have you been doing?
You'll be sleeping with Mamaw, Elmo'll have the front bedroom, so
try to slip in and not wake her up."

She tiptoed into her room to get her pajamas. Mamaw was sleeping
in the middle of the bed with her mouth hanging open, toothless and
dark. Changing in the bathroom, she glanced furtively at her
nakedness. It seemed very important just then. It was real, and all this
other stuff just a jumble. She was pleased with her breasts and their
pink, tight nipples, and touched one of them with the tip of her finger,
then guiltily took it away. It was still a stranger's body. She pulled her
pajamas on quickly to hide it.

When she came out, her mother was waiting in the hall and followed her into the bedroom. In bed, she lay far over to the side to
avoid contact with Mamaw. Edna Earle knelt down beside her and
began talking, asking questions. Her breath blew disagreeably into
Lori's face, taking her own breath away. She began to talk about
Duane and Randy in a menacing, vague way. Boys that age get
strange ideas about girls, she said. Sometimes they want to touch
them or sometimes they just look at them a certain way. Sometimes
they say bad words, and a nice girl mustn't listen. You can't be too
careful. Duane and Randy might not be very nice. She'd better stay
away from them.

She went on and on, her voice droning in warning and asking if
anything had happened today or if there was anything she wanted to
ask about all that. Prying, probing, her breath blowing sweet and per-
fumy. Her mouth was a bright red pointed bow. Lori would have bit-
ten her own tongue off before she'd have asked her anything.

And still she went on. Why the Lord made it so there had to be all that before people could have babies she'd never know. And now her precious girl having to grow up to all that. It broke her heart to think about it. She wished she could think Lori would never have anything to do with boys, not ever.

Lori held herself very still and narrow between the old woman in the bed and her mother kneeling beside her on the floor and crying now a little.

VI

COMING AWAKE THE NEXT MORNING, still more than half asleep, not yet thinking and remembering everything from the night before, Lori was aware first of being sweaty, then of unaccustomed voices in the other part of the house, then, opening her eyes, of a dark cavern of a mouth and a stale smell where only an empty white pillow should have been. She rolled away and out of bed, half-falling on the floor. Then she shook herself awake and it came back. Mamaw, of course; she had been put there for the night.

No one cared about *her*, of course; it was *her* bed, but no one cared about that, they just invaded it whenever they felt like it. Scowling, feeling put upon and out of sorts and resentful, she looked back. Mamaw's filmed, watery eyes were fixed on her accusingly—as if *she* were the interloper!

"I thought you never was going to wake up so I could roll over," she complained. "I'm all stiff from laying one way." Her empty lips worked in and out as she spoke. She turned herself in the bed and threw a sparsely haired leg out from under the sheet. "As soon as you get your clothes on, tell Edna Earle I want my coffee."

Lori went off to the bathroom in a fury. Mamaw had no right to intrude, to look at her and touch flesh with her when she was half asleep and full-bladdered and vulnerable. No one did. She slouched into the kitchen in her tackiest shorts and top, hair uncombed. When she got a hard look from her mother for her trouble, she felt doubly mistreated.

The aunts were gathering again to decide what to do about Mamma. Dr. Kneeland had said she couldn't be left alone, not for a while at least, and who was going to take her? They sat around the table in sober conference. Lori saw that if she wanted any breakfast she would have to get it herself.

When she remembered to pass on the message about Mamaw's coffee, her mother heaved a great sigh and looked at Ruth and Cleora: that was how it was going to be, wait on her hand and foot. Lori's feelings hardened against them all. Forgetting for the moment that she had been resenting Mamaw, too, she thought how mean and stingy

Mama was being. Aunt Billie wouldn't have acted like that. She would have been glad to take Mamaw what she wanted, and would have said good morning and tried to cheer her up. "She only wanted some coffee!" she hurled at them. "Is that so much?"

They stared at her. Who was this smart-mouthed kid that had appeared in their midst and taken the place of that good little girl?

Later, Edna Earle shoved a list and some money into Lori's hand and sent her off to the grocery store. They were all going to be there for lunch, she said, to decide some things. She guessed people thought she didn't have a thing to do but cook for an army. She was flushed and damp, all in a fluster. "And get yourself into something decent before you go," she told her. "I don't know what on earth you were thinking of, putting on those things! Cleora must think I let you run wild."

Lori wasn't about to change clothes. Aunt Cleora, she said to herself, could think whatever she liked. She waited until her mother was busy again and wouldn't notice, then marched defiantly off in her shorts.

As it turned out, her mother was right, or maybe the way she was dressed was irrelevant and it would have happened anyway. John Pollard, who worked at the grocery store nearby, tucked up his apron when he saw her and walked her home. It was about the most romantic thing that had ever happened to Lori; she was stricken dumb with self-consciousness. And if that weren't enough, when they were about a block from the store a carload of boys passed and whistled, then circled the block and cruised by again. This time when the car drew even with them, it slowed, and one of the boys yelled out the window a resounding "Fuck!"

She was mortified just at the sound of it. That awful, forbidden word! She felt threatened and soiled, as if they had scrawled it across her face the way people scrawled it on underpasses and restroom booths. She tried to keep walking, to act as though nothing had happened, but she couldn't. John Pollard was telling her not to worry about it, not to let it bother her, that all it showed was how rude and crude those guys were. Yet something had come into his face, she didn't know what exactly, but some look of sly satisfaction. She just wished he would shut up! He ought to pretend he hadn't heard, instead of going on and on like that. It was too much. She snatched her bag of groceries, wheeled, and ran up a driveway, right into the back yard of the house they were passing. There she hid behind a bank of honeysuckle until she was sure he was gone, then, shaken, picked her way home through back yards and alleys.

The house was as crowded as it had been the night before. She shut herself in her closet and changed into her plainest skirt and blouse, but even there she couldn't let herself cry because there would be no way to keep them all from seeing when she came out. They were all there, every one of them, even Uncle Floyd's wife and Albert Barnes and Aunt Ora Lee's odd, demented-looking little girl. They all kept complaining about the heat, while Edna Earle explained over and over that it was Mamma who claimed she couldn't stand the cooler. But after lunch (with people sitting all over the house and to Lori's astonishment even daring to take messy chocolate pie into the forbidden living room), when they were ready to get down to some serious talking, they turned on the cooler anyway, to keep Mamma from hearing what was said.

Then there was another scene as ugly as the one at the park, or uglier, with accusations all around and squabbling over money and no one willing to take Mamma. Billie went back and forth taking her a tray and seeing if she needed anything, mainly just talking to her and making sure she didn't feel abandoned back there, trying to keep her from being upset by the fuss going on in the other room. Finally, when things got really nasty, she broke out crying and asked didn't anybody care about poor Mamma and what she wanted? She asked Lori to take over checking on her then, so Mamma wouldn't see that she had been crying.

Finally it was decided, as everyone had known it would be, that Edna Earle would take her. No one else would agree to except Billie, who had only a little garage apartment that wouldn't do at all because of the stairs, if nothing else. The others were all to send a certain amount of money every month. So it was settled, and they all left about half mad at all the others, and Lori was left facing a home with Mamaw there all the time and feeling her life permanently invaded.

At least Mamaw moved into the spare bedroom and she got her own room back—for all the good that did her, since no one ever bothered to knock. But even so, it was an invasion. She needed a private place where she could set up her defenses against the assault of huge troubles: feet too big, hair too straight, pimples, chronic tongue-tie in the presence of any male under forty. There was no room in her life just then for patience with Mamaw. She couldn't stand her nasty spit can and her odor of stale urine, her unwelcome bits of obsolete wisdom. She couldn't stand her pouting fits, the way she screwed her mouth into a knot and sat around with her chin in her hand.

She couldn't stand her mother, either. Edna Earle took pride, the pride of martyrdom, in being the only one to do her duty by Mamma. She told everyone who would listen that she owed it to her and would never ever be willing to see her mother want for proper care. At the same time, she resented everything she did for her. During the weeks Mamaw was off her feet after the stroke, Edna Earle complained that she expected her to come sit in there and talk to her during the day. How could she get her housework done if she did that? And when she was able to be up and around again Edna Earle complained that she got in the way, especially trying to help with things when she couldn't. It drove her crazy. And the mess! Not only was there that awful spit can, but Mamma tended to leak on her way to the toilet, so she had to keep washing up spots on the bathroom floor several times a day. And then, too, there was that awful bird.

"That awful bird" was a yellow canary Lori had bought Mamaw for Christmas several years ago with her saved-up allowance money. Naturally the bird moved in when Mamaw did. As far as Lori was concerned, Petey was the only good part of the situation. When she came in from school every day, she went in to trade whistles with him. She did all the changing of paper in the bottom of the cage and the filling of food cups and water cups. Edna Earle never had to do a thing that way. But Petey was incorrigibly addicted to throwing seeds on the floor from the metal tray-table where his cage sat, and that was enough to make him a nuisance. For Edna Earle, Petey summed up all the hardship and trouble Mamma's presence in the house was causing her.

For Lori, the inconvenience was rather more than taking on additional chores. Where once she had surrounded Mamaw's past with a haze of historic glamour, so that Mamaw herself assumed the dimensions of heroism, she now saw only the ugly things of the present. She was ashamed of her. How could she have friends in when there sat Mamaw like Poe's raven, quothing at them? What good would it have done if the very captain of the football team had given her a second glance?

Not that she would have been any shining social success anyway.

She never had been. But she had never before cared. Now she discovered that she was not only a loner, but lonely. She was withdrawn and all but friendless; people said she was stuck-up. She longed for boyfriends but walked between classes with her eyes on her shoes, and in study hall she studied. Or read, actually; she didn't do anything that might improve her grades, which after years of straight A's had plummeted. After years, too, of outward docility, she had launched a war of resistance against everything—mainly, that is, against her mother. All in all, it was turning out to be a bad year. It would have been anyway, even without Mamaw. She felt like a hodgepodge of persons, separate elements contending for dominance, and she never knew which one would turn up on top at any given moment. All that would have been true anyway. But it was easy to convince herself that the problem was all Mamaw.

Part of it was that Edna Earle had social ambitions for her. She urged her to make friends among "that Arlington Heights bunch at church"; to "act cuter" around people her own age; to show an interest in lots of boys, not just John Pollard. "Don't waste your time with him," she said. "His people aren't worth two cents, none of those Church of God people are." (He was, for a fact, a splinter-sect fundamentalist and conspicuously pious, even preachy.) She exhorted Lori to join Youth for Christian Living and, in the same breath, to play her cards right and get a husband who had a little something instead of one who would just get by all their lives. She made her enter the Posture Queen competition, and Lori had to walk across the stage in front of the whole school in her gym suit, slumping miserably to hide the yet unaccustomed protuberances in front, caught between embarrassment that they should be there at all and shame that they were not larger. She stopped Lori's piano lessons because people didn't want to hear that kind of music anyway, and enrolled her in tap dancing so she could be in the school shows. "It must feel so great to be up there in front of everyone, in your costume and the lights on you. I want you to do all those things I never had a chance to do."

E. Z. enjoined Lori privately to pay no attention to her, but otherwise stayed out of it.

Nearly every night at bedtime she was in Lori's room with some sermon or other. Being more outgoing was a constant theme, and posture, and keeping up on studies but not being a bookworm, and going out for cheerleader. And sex, always the evils of sex. She harangued Lori with so many warnings about the evil impulses of boys ("They're all out to get whatever they can from you!") that she was too paralyzed with anxiety to act natural if a boy so much as spoke to her.

Then, late in the fall, the calls started coming. Once or twice a week, the whispering voice with its obscene proposals, its offers and descriptions and questions about her body, her underwear. Often Edna Earle would answer the telephone, then smile and nod encouragement while handing her the receiver, and she would have to pretend to be talking about something, while the whisper went on. The worst part was being afraid whoever it was on the telephone would approach her at school and she would have to look at him and think of those words he had said. Or, no, really the worst part was being unable to make the words he whispered—somehow she knew instinctively, at once, what they meant, even the words she had never heard before—to make them and the pictures they created stop going through and through her mind. There was one phrase that particularly haunted her: "Somebody'll get to you before you're fifteen."

She needed to talk to someone, some woman, but there seemed to be no one she could talk to. There was, of course; there was Aunt Billie. But at the time Lori thought she couldn't possibly repeat the words, even to her. She was afraid that if she did Aunt Billie would frown and blame her, somehow, she didn't know for what.

Everything was wrong, and there was no getting away. Not at school, and certainly not at home, where the calls kept coming and the problem of Mamaw was all-present. When she came home, there was Mamaw sitting humped over and sour in her chair. When she went to bed at night, there beyond the door the squabbling and the whining continued.

One night she was lying in bed full of tears that she was trying, with everything she had, to hold back. She clenched her fists and swore to herself that she would never be like them, not either one of them. Then Mamaw appeared in the rectangle of light at the half-open door, shaking off support and jerking away the night-gown Edna Earle was holding up for her. She wasn't a baby, she said. She could still do for herself. She stood in her baggy knee-length drawers, bracing her legs like wooden stilts, staggering a little, the gown aloft now and twisted about her head. Her empty old tits hung long and flat toward her belly.

VII

THE BOYS HAD SAID, come to see us, come for a visit. And Aunt Ruth had said it, too, had seconded it, when they gathered the day after the picnic to decide what to do with Mamma. Lori put it to Edna Earle right then: "I can go, can't I, Mamma?" Edna Earle bit her lip and smiled falsely: "We'll see." For there were the boys, wild things, the enemy; you could never tell what they might say or show to an innocent girl. Then in the worry and trouble of Mamaw's illness the idea was dropped.

Now, a year later, in spite of her mother's misgivings and objections, Lori was setting out to make that visit, retracing on a Greyhound bus the road by which they had come twenty-five years before.

It had been such a bad year, in every way. The only good thing about it had been that Mamaw's presence brought Aunt Billie around more often. She came once a week, "to help with Mamma," she said, then spent the day sitting at the kitchen table, drinking Cokes and laughing and teasing. Well, that was a kind of helping, or it could have been if Edna Earle had let it. Mamaw always brightened up when Billie was around. "That little mess," she called her. As often as she could, Lori contrived to have a headache or sore throat on the days of Billie's visits. She loved her laugh and the way she threw her hands through her hair, never caring which way it settled. She loved her amused and easy way of telling about Garth's and his friends' exploits.

About three Billie would look at the clock and say she'd better go so she'd be home when Garth got there. She always kissed Mamaw good-bye and gave Lori a wink, inviting her to be a coconspirator against the somber powers. After she left Edna Earle always spoke darkly about Billie's having a good heart but no judgment and about having rescued Billie from some dire moral fate on the order of Ora Lee's. In return Billie had ungratefully thrown herself away on that ball player.

It infuriated Lori that she should talk about Billie that way. It seemed to her that Aunt Billie wasn't thrown away at all. She thought that she and Garth were good together, and good for each other. She even suspected that whatever Aunt Billie had with Garth was part of what made her so different from Mama, so much more alive. What she sensed from her aunt was that a man, a connection with a man, could be a positive thing after all, something happy and sustaining— though all the rest of the evidence was against it.

Things with Mamaw got worse and worse. Even by Christmas it was obvious that the arrangement wasn't working, but no one knew what else to do. She was too feeble to live alone anymore. Cleora tried taking her but brought her back after three days, saying the house smelled. By that time there were hard feelings all around.

Then in March, Ruth surprised everyone by offering to take her down there "if it could be worked out"—meaning if everyone would kick in a certain amount every month to make it worth her while. Dr. Kneeland was consulted on whether she could stand the trip, the others were pressed to agree, and Ruth and Jess came and got her.

It was a blustery, damp March day, and depressing, with Billie there crying and blowing her nose and Lori feeling all kinds of regret and guilt for not having treated Mamaw better. Ruth and Jess drove in late in the morning, ate a quick lunch, and loaded for the trip back. There wasn't much to load. Everything she was taking, nearly everything she owned, went in one suitcase: a few dresses and nightgowns, drawers and stockings and two slips, an extra pair of shoes, medicine. After lunch they put her coat around her and got her into the back seat. Edna Earle put in an old pillow for her, and she lay down across the seat with her knees drawn up, making a hollow for the canary's square cage. Her filmed old eyes were far away and her mouth set.

It was then, just as they were ready to back out, that Aunt Ruth revitalized the seed that had been planted the previous summer. She stuck her round head out the car window and called back, "Lori, honey, now don't you forget you said you'd come see us. Your Mamaw's goin' to miss you, remember."

Even then she might not have thought any more about it if other things had not gone so badly. Mainly, it was the dirty telephone calls. She had been needing so badly to have someone to talk to about them, and there had seemed to be no one. Her only close friend, fat Elaine, would have giggled and thought it was exciting. Besides that, she would have told. But the calls kept coming, and Lori was bothered, upset. So for lack of anyone else, John Pollard, still hanging around in a semi-boyfriendly way, became her confidant. He made her tell the very words, and she was miserably embarrassed, but he took such a high-minded approach that it had to be all right. Preachy as ever, he went on and on about keeping a pure mind and being above all that. He even quoted Scripture.

Then one night when a call came there was a mix-up about who was taking the phone, herself or her mother, and in the confusion the caller spoke to her in his natural voice, instead of the ugly whisper. It was John Pollard. She couldn't believe it—but she had to believe it. To think of the things she had told him! He must have been laughing at her all the time.

That was when she revived the idea of a visit to Aunt Ruth's. She had to get away. Down in East Texas, down home, all these terrible things that had made it so bad a year wouldn't exist. Aunt Ruth would be kind to Mamaw, the cousins and their friends would think she was fine just as she was, and no one would make demands or exert pressures.

But when she mentioned it, there was a great row, a series of great rows. Edna Earle used every argument. She would get down there and be so bored she wouldn't know what to do. E. Z. would be gone at the same time—whatever time it was—and she didn't want to be alone. Most important, there were the boys, the cousins; they were so wild, no telling what they might do. There were arguments between Edna Earle and E. Z. Why not? he said, and she said it was out of the question. But finally (though he was not accustomed to stepping in and settling things and though he himself would not willingly have spent one day within a fifty-mile radius of Ruth and Jess's place in piney, sandy Red River County), he said, "If she wants to go that much, then by God she's going."

So it was settled. But privately he, too, asked her why she wanted to go. She couldn't say. She brushed off even the need to have a reason, as if she had always been going off to visit country aunts in the summer. When pressed, she said she wanted to see Mamaw. "Don't you think she'd like for me to come and see her?" After all, she had always been the favorite grandchild.

So in July, just after her fifteenth birthday, with a suitcase full of new birthday clothes, she went off on her first trip alone. Edna Earle resisted to the end. If she had to go, they could at least drive her. But Lori insisted that it was to be her own trip, made on her own. When E. Z. backed her in that, too, Edna Earle accused him of being irresponsible and not caring what might happen. But he held firm, and when the day arrived he was the one who drove her to the bus station. To Lori, it seemed like a very special thing, to get away just the two of them and even have breakfast at the station.

Outside it was an ordinary July morning, the sky empty and far, the sun beating down, heat shimmers rising from the pavement. But the coffee shop was moistly cool from the evaporative air conditioning, and travellers or just passersby who wanted to share the coolness exchanged low monosyllables over their Saturday morning coffee. Lori had coffee, too—another first—in honor of the occasion. She took minute sips and watched her father over the rim. The steaming illicit brew, illicit because Edna Earle disapproved of coffee drinking, made them feel like conspirators against some mutual oppressor.

E. Z. talked about the special virtue or dignity that writers had thought belonged to country life, or to the South. He fancied himself a fair amateur historian, and the South was his specialty. He wasn't sure all that was true, himself, he said. She looked out at the few people on the quiet Saturday street and wondered what he was getting at. Finally he cleared his throat and said he hoped she'd have a good time. It didn't seem like the kind of thing she'd enjoy, but how did he know? He paused and scratched his ankle, trying to seem casual, and they looked at each other uncomfortably. They were not used to talking like this, and the moment seemed to demand something adequate.

"What I want to say is this," he went on. "I have a lot of confidence that you'll figure out things your own way and make up your own mind. That's what I want you to do. Like this trip now. I'm sure you have your own reasons for wanting to go, even if you can't say them in so many words, and whatever they are, they're not the reasons your mother thinks you have or the ones she would have herself."

"Oh—her!"

"Now, now, okay. Never mind. You just go down there and size things up for yourself, and think things over, whatever it is that you need to think over. I guess that's all I wanted to say."

Out in the departure area, a roofed concrete gulf, the noise of motors blocked out all other sound. He put her suitcase down beside the steps of the bus and leaned over to shout into her ear, "Be careful, now." She started to get on, but he pulled her back to kiss her forehead. Then she wanted to stop and tell him about the calls, about everything, but there was no time and the noise was too much.

Clutching her library books, the history he had checked out for her and the novel she had checked out for herself, she climbed aboard.

Latecomers got on and stowed their things on the overhead rack. A woman took the seat beside her. The driver swung into his seat and closed the door. He started the motor, touched all the switches and knobs around the dash and the seat with quick, testing gestures, and pulled in grinding low gear to the driveway, then out into the street. Lori waved back to her dad, standing in the driveway with his hands in his pockets, looking after her as they pulled away.

As she watched the shabbier side of downtown Fort Worth slip past —used furniture stores, broken curbs and gravel parking lots, an old red stone church building converted to a tire store with tires stacked high showing through the colored windows—she was struck by the raw ugliness of it. Why was it so important to her mother to have reached this place? She was glad to be escaping it.

Scalding sun poured over the silver Greyhound and rebounded off its ridged hide. Heat shimmers advanced to meet them on the highway. Her seatmate remarked that it must be a hundred and five. She was an open-faced woman wearing a tacky print dress, with bare feet shoved into high-heeled shoes. Her hair was the thin, dyed-black kind that roaches back from the forehead and turns up in splitting curls at the ends. After a few minutes, when Lori didn't answer, the woman added complacently, "Yes, we are flat goin' to melt in this thing." She fanned herself with what looked like a shirt cardboard. "You goin' far, honey?"

"East Texas," she said. She looked out the window, wanting to use her time for watching and thinking, not talking.

"My, that's nice." She went into a long narrative of her own girlhood in East Texas. Lori nodded now and then at the appropriate places.

East Texas. East Texas. As far back as she could remember, the phrase had stood for not just a place, the region lying somewhere east of Dallas and south of Oklahoma, but for a condition, a different kind of life, the past surviving, with some modulations, into the present. "East Texas" and "down home": they went together.

While the woman beside her rattled on, she looked out at the small and weedy plots where a cow or two dozed or patches of corn turned to rattling stalks under the July sun. Even her imagination could not turn these into vestiges of that austere and hearty world that had once seemed to open to her through the faces in the family portrait. A half-acre cow lot was still just a cow lot. But the country retreat waiting for her at the end of her bus ride would be different. She would be able to invest it with all the undevious and unambitious and, yes, unsexed bareness of the past. Was it a time or a place she wanted to find? She didn't know. The two were mixed up together. She just wanted something different from what she'd had.

She watched the places stream past the window. They had escaped Fort Worth some time ago and skirted Dallas, eluded it. She watched the names float by on the highway signs and railway depots: Rockwall, Greenville, Commerce. What dusty little towns! All trucks and barefoot children and straw hats. She threw their names away. One of them had a big sign, like a welcome banner, high across the road at the edge of town, a portal for all to pass under: THE BLACKEST LAND AND THE WHITEST PEOPLE.

After that she tried to read for a while, but her eyes kept lifting to the miles slipping past. She was impatient for her raucous cousins, good-hearted boys, she was sure, and for plain Aunt Ruth and the old house with its board floors, for Mamaw, for a special look of land to replace these ragged fields.

"Someone'll get to you before you're fifteen." Well, she had tricked him, she had tricked them all. She had turned fifteen, and she was still intact, ungotten.

At Paris her seatmate got off and went away with another woman and a couple of towheaded little boys. Lori had to change buses, and to kill the half-hour wait she walked twice around the square. It was not a town she could like. There was a Woolworth's, a Lerner's, a Star movie. She was glad to find her bus and read until it pulled out, stopped for a few seconds at a dim traffic light, and turned onto the narrow blacktop road to Clamie.

It was that road that she had imagined to be her bridge to the authentic past, her escape route from complications to simplicity, even security. She closed the book of dead Southern heroism that her father had chosen for her and looked out eagerly at the real and sandy corn fields and cotton fields, the men in trucks waiting at the side roads for the bus to pass. When she stepped down in front of the drugstore in Clamie, they were waiting for her, broad-faced Aunt Ruth and comical, scrawny Jess, looking nothing at all like *American Gothic*.

VIII

THE OLD PLYMOUTH WAS WAITING, and they drove through Clamie, past its pair of filling stations, low-marqueed movie house, feed store, dry goods store, two or three cafes. Aunt Ruth talked in a steady stream: How was Edna Earle? How as E. Z.? Was it fun going so far alone? Jess said nothing. He drove as if he had just learned that week, gripping the steering wheel with both hands, stiff armed and grim, ready for the machine to run out from under him or crash into a post.

Their house was about a mile outside the tattered fringe of town, not the old house Lori had visited as a child, but one very much like it, with boards worn a silky gray. A gravel driveway ran past the house to a leaning garage in back, but no one ever bothered putting a car in it. The front yard, on both sides of the driveway and all across its front half, was rutted and packed from being driven over and parked on. A battered black pickup some way off the gravel had the look of a vehicle not moved in a long time. Weeds luxuriated under and around it.

Aunt Ruth said, "Here we are, honey," and told her to go on in, Mamaw was in the front bedroom.

She pushed through a creaking screen door into the front room, with two chairs and a wooden-armed couch covered with a printed cotton throw, partly tucked in at the crevices and partly not. A box of Eagle dominoes stood ready for action on the step end table, a card table propped against the wall. Perfect, she thought; comfortable looking. A house where all the rooms were open for use and the furniture was meant to be sat on.

From the next room she heard Mamaw's voice, talking, hesitating, talking. She hadn't heard her come in. Lori slipped to the door and looked in. She sat in a slat rocker with a granny-square afghan partly drawn around her shoulders, looking thin and more deeply eroded than ever. Her hands picked fretfully at real or imagined bits on her lap, on the chair arm. "Seems like time she oughta be here," she complained. She bent, picked up her can and spat, wiped her mouth with the back of her hand, and resumed a slight rocking. A brown line ran down her chin.

She was talking to the canary.

"Here I am, Mamaw," Lori said, and went to her chair.

She caught Lori's hand, then her shoulder, and pulled her down close. Again that familiar smell, the smell of bad gums and leaky bladder and stale snuff. She squinted critically. "Lipstick! I swan!"

Lori told her she was looking good and squeezed her hand. The canary hopped about his cage: upper left to lower right to lower left; reverse and pick a seed; drop; reverse; lower left to upper right; chirp. He kept his black bead of an eye on Lori. She asked how he was, if he liked it here.

"Hmmp. Nobody likes it here. They just drug me off down here and put me in jail." She complained of the food, the raw milk, the radio stations that never got the ball games. But yes, Petey had been all right. He didn't sing much anymore, though. She sighed heavily. "I guess Petey's gettin' old, too. And them boys, in and out all hours, wakin' him up. I can't never get a decent night's sleep for them boys and all their cars. In and out, in and out."

Lori saw Aunt Ruth in the doorway and knew she must have heard, but it didn't seem to matter. She smiled—a settled expression with her, as if she had only to relax her face from any more urgent purpose and it would settle into that wide smile, a gap in her roundness. "That shows she's feelin' good," she said. "If she can fuss, you know she's all right. You want to see the rest of the place, honey?"

Opening directly off the small front bedroom, which housed a variety of boxes and miscellaneous objects as well as Mamaw, was the square, multipurpose dining room, then the kitchen, also big and square with doors opening off in various directions. Across the back of the house a deep screened-in porch with a few knocked-about chairs and a glider looked out at a solitary cow and a sun-dried garden.

A washtub of freshly picked black-eyed peas occupied the center of the porch. They were the last for the year, Aunt Ruth said. She rambled on about the garden, the weather. She didn't know where the boys were, never did know for sure. She looked pleased at their resourcefulness in eluding her.

Lori looked out the back door. What next? It was three in the afternoon, and she had just gotten here, and she didn't know what to do till supper. She surprised herself by asking if she could help with anything.

Aunt Ruth surprised her more by accepting. "I did have in mind shelling them peas," she said. "We'll have some at dinner tomorrow, and I'll put up the rest." She handed Lori a pan and said she'd go get Mamma to come and help, too. "She'd never hear me from here," she said. "She can't hear a thing unless she wants to."

Lori had never shelled peas—she had never done much of anything in the way of work—and she found that it wasn't as easy as it looked. Her pile of hulls grew slowly while theirs mounted right up. They snapped the end, pulled the string, and zipped out all the brown-eyed yellow green peas with their clinging bits of white gauze, all in one motion, while she broke, broke, broke each pod and shucked out one pea at a time. It was peculiarly satisfying when, once in a great while, she did lay open the whole long case with its entire little freight. But then she saw that tiny worms peeked out of some of them, and she picked furtively back through her cone of shelled peas in case she had already missed some.

Mamaw stopped every couple of minutes to rub and stretch her hands. Shelling peas cramped them, she said. But she didn't talk much, not like she used to. Aunt Ruth did that. She had turned now to trivia about Duane and Randy's friends, what they said and wore and how they cut up and how they all hated school. Sometimes Mamaw scowled or muttered to herself in the middle of it. At first Lori thought she was listening and expressing disapproval, but then she realized that her mind was wandering. Once she put in crankily, "Well, I don't see why Edna Earle had to put up them new curtains. The old ones was plenty good." Aunt Ruth shook her head significantly and stifled a giggle, but to Lori it seemed very sad. She had somehow imagined that being down here would restore Mamaw, but already she could see that instead she had declined.

Jess came around the side of the house with a can of motor oil and a rag. He hawked and spat, then came up the back steps, grinned at Lori, and sat down to nap in the slat rocker. It was hot. Her sweated blouse stuck to her back, and she was beginning to feel cramped from sitting in one position. She told Aunt Ruth she thought she'd go look out back, and got up and stretched.

She walked past soft black piles, where flies were busy, to where the cow was eating dry grass in a ring at the limit of her rope. There was nothing else. Except for infrequent cars on the road there was no sound but the cow's brushing through the dry grass and the rip of her teeth. It was all stasis and dryness and dead heat.

When she came back, the boys had come in. Seeing Lori, they stopped firing shelled peas at each other long enough to say hey, then went back to it. Their real business, though, was trying to tease a dollar out of Aunt Ruth. She chuckled and shook her head no, but they kept at it, calling her Old Moneybags and whatever else they could think of. "Them boys is going to dollar you to death," Mamaw told her, but none of them paid any attention. Finally they clenched their case by saying that after all they wouldn't need show money tonight because they were going to drive Lori around some with Jerry. Ruth said that was real nice, and gave them a dollar apiece.

Sure enough, after supper they told Lori to hurry up, ol' Jerry was probably out there already. They stomped up and down the front porch while she put on a sun dress and lipstick. When she went out, ol' Jerry was indeed sitting slumped under the wheel, waiting. All she could tell about him was that he was long and lean, with a shock of black hair. They jammed her in the middle between him and Duane, with Randy hanging over their shoulders from the back, and they were off on the grand tour. Back through Clamie, up and down the main drag, waving and saying hey to anyone under age twenty-five, and then out the highway toward Clarksville. They had been riding a quarter hour or more when Duane remembered to say, "Oh yeah, Lori this is Jerry."

After that, Jerry began to risk a look at her now and then, and she began to think of things to say. They rode around the square in Clarksville, but there was hardly anyone on the street. They must all be at the movie, the boys said. They should have gone themselves. But maybe they could go to the midweek show in Clamie Thursday night. Jerry agreed, and asked Lori if she wanted to.

This was going splendidly! She had only gotten there that afternoon, and already she had a date.

On the drive back, Jerry stretched his arm along the back of the seat behind her shoulders. He apologized for not driving her down to Talco to see the oil wells, but he had to get the car back by 8:30. He dropped them all in front of the house and said, "See you tomorrow," and roared off.

"Told you you'd like ol' Jerry," Randy commented.

Inside, Ruth and Jess were playing forty-two with some neighbors.

Mamaw sat just inside the door of her room, watching and spitting. "I sure am glad you're back," she told Lori. "I don't know why you had to go off and leave me, just to go ridin' with them boys." Duane said that maybe she liked boys better'n old ladies, and Randy broke up laughing. She rocked on, sullenly, and wouldn't even look at them.

The dominoes clacked together. A moth circled the dim yellow light above the table. The boys walked back and forth, fidgeted. After a while they poked Jess's arm and asked for the car keys.

"Now, boys," he told them slowly, never taking his eyes off the dominoes. "You know I told you you'd done burnt up all the gas I was buyin' you for this week."

"Come on, there ain't nothin' to do here."

He fished in his pocket, clapped the keys down on the corner of the table, and went on playing. "Where'd you say you was goin'?"

"Didn't say."

"We might go look for ol' Debbie Ann, or Wanda maybe."

The neighbors laughed knowingly, and called after them, "You better stay away from them two."

From the other room Mamaw called Lori to come read her a chapter. She had moved out of the light to let her hair down and brush it, piling the gray-white puffs in her lap. "Nobody ever will," she complained, "and at least on Saturday night and Sunday I love to hear a chapter read. We always used to have a chapter on Saturday night before bed. Boys didn't go runnin' around free as they pleased back then."

So Lori read Matthew 10, and then sat with her by the radio and started over on the book her dad had checked out for her. After a while she put that one away and got out the novel she had checked out for herself in the adult section. *Lamb in His Bosom*, it was called. She was reading it only when no one was around to look over her shoulder. Next she wanted to read *Grapes of Wrath*, which Elaine Tuttle had said was forbidden to her.

The dominoes clacked.

After an hour the boys rushed back in, demanding to take the pickup now. "What you want that for?" Jess asked. "Anyway, it's about outa gas." But they said they would put in a couple of gallons. Duane rummaged in the hall closet and pulled out a quilt. When Ruth asked what that was for, he told her never mind and with a sly look added that he'd already told her they were going to look for ol' Debbie

Ann.

"Now I told you to stay away from them two girls," she scolded. "You better not be cookin' up any nastiness, you hear? Wantin' quilts and the truck! I won't have that, now." It was easy to see she was only playing a game with them.

"Course not," Duane said. He cut his eyes toward Randy and grinned.

"You have them girls with you?" she demanded.

"Naw, not with us. They're outside in the truck."

They went out brazenly flaunting the quilt, tussling and grinning. One of the neighbors called after them that they'd better watch out or they might bring home something they didn't want. Nobody seemed bothered about it. Lori didn't know whether to believe them or to think it was all a fake and they were just bragging.

"Them boys," Mamaw lamented, "them and their nastiness. And that Ruth just eggs 'em on. I wouldn't a-thought I'd see the day." She shook her head, her mouth drawn up in a tight knot.

In the other room, Aunt Ruth, too, was saying, "Them boys! I swear, if they ain't somethin'." She giggled, and went on playing forty-two.

Sunday morning was church, with a great bustle of getting ready. Aunt Ruth, in a jersey print, was corseted to blocky splendor, and old Jess was grave in rusty black and string tie. The boys were on their best behavior. Only Mamaw stayed at home, pottering about in her nightgown for a while and then sinking into her rocking chair. She just didn't feel like getting out, she said.

The preacher waved his arms and shouted down sin in a more uninhibited fashion than Lori was used to, and twice there were amens from the front pews, but otherwise it was pretty much the same as it was at home. At last, after "Bringing in the Sheaves" failed to bring any fresh sheaves up the aisle into the preacher's barn, the congregation broke into family units again and made for the door. "Edna Earle's girl, this is Edna Earle's girl," Aunt Ruth said, over and over.

Lori had already asked about Uncle Elmo, where he lived and whether he ever came to visit. She would like to see him while she was here, she said. So after dinner they decided to drive out to his place.

Mamaw had gone back to bed and had taken her meal there, but when she heard where they were going nothing would do but she would get up and go along. She and Ruth squabbled over it for a good

five minutes, how if a person didn't feel like getting up to eat she sure
didn't feel like going somewhere in the car and how a mother had a
right to go see her own son if she wanted to. It ended with a com-
promise agreement that she would not dress or get out, but would ride
with them in her housecoat and sit in the car while they walked
around.

"Ain't nobody offered to take *me* out there the whole time I been
here," she grumbled.

It seemed to Lori that they must have made a dozen turns on narrow
back roads when Ruth pointed out the old home place, standing at a
perilous tilt with its flank to the road, long empty and weathered
almost black. Just after they passed it they made the last turn and they
were there.

At Elmo's all was quiet. A patch of weeds in front of the house had
been left to grow tall. Two or three dingy white hens fluffed
themselves in the dust of the beaten dirt trail that ran as a driveway
across the front and down the side, where it widened into a catchall
area toward the back. Except for the chickens, the place looked
deserted, less alive than the dark pine woods encircling it.

Jess thought Elmo might have gone to Jake Glover's grave. But after
they stopped and got out, with a slamming of doors, he came slipping
around one end of the house, slack of trouser and shifty-eyed. He
shook hands ceremoniously with Jess, and nodded to Ruth and Lori,
then stood with his right elbow winged, as if he had started to put his
hand in his pocket but had given up the idea partway. After a minute
he said, "H'lo, Mamma, how are you?"

Jess asked him how things were going, and they looked around a little. But Elmo said that it was really the old home place that Lori ought
to see, if she wanted to. So they settled it that he would bring her
home later on in his wagon, and the two of them struck out past the
littered fenced area where Adam, his old spotted-on-white horse,
stood dozing with one hoof hiked.

At the edge of the garden he paused, indicating the remnants of his
summer's vegetables apologetically. "Mamma always had a fine
garden," he said. "We never was short of what to eat." Lori said that
her mother had told her that. "Talks about it like she misses it, does
she?" That was hard to answer truthfully. "Sort of," she said.

Behind the garden were dried-up patches of corn and cotton, then a
fence and uncultivated fields belonging to the home place. They stood

together looking at it, a space grown up in weeds with pine woods curving around to hold it in an arc, no life anywhere in it.

He held the strands of wire apart for her, and they walked through the high grass. They must have played hide and seek in this field, she thought, all those years ago. She tried to imagine herself one of them, running across that very field and squealing, playing tag, careless of clothes or noise. The sun was very bright. When she squinted, it flashed between her lashes and turned the brown field gold. Grasshoppers whirred all around her and rode on the dry tips of grasses.

"You oughtn't to worn those open shoes and bare legs," Elmo said. "I remember when your mother got bit by a copperhead once, not in this field but in the next one. Caught her under the toe when she was puttin' her foot down on it. Oh, it was bad. Her poor leg swole up double and turned all mottled. Mamma had me kill a chicken and put the hot innards on it to draw the poison, then egg whites after that."

They passed through a narrow belt of woods, walking on pine needles, and crossed another field of high grass, like the first but bigger. He showed her where the barn and sheds had been, but there was no sign of them now. They walked all around the old house. Up close, she could see that the roof had caved in and the porch floor was rotted out. Better not try to go in, he said. But he found a thick limb for her to stand on, and carried it for her from window to low window so she could look in. What was that strange looking cabinet thing in the corner? Her Mamaw's kitchen safe, he said, or one of 'em. She had wanted so bad to take them with her to Fort Worth, but Buford wouldn't. Lori looked in at it. The door was rusted off, but leaned neatly against the cabinet.

They talked about why Mamaw had left and the troubles there had been, with Ora Lee, with Jake Glover. She tried to picture to herself the things he talked about, the dead chickens on the porch and the broken windows, the fire at the other house. Even more she tried to picture the good times before. She saw them brown and hard and healthy, and Mamaw tall, standing on the top step of this porch with one long hand on the post (that post there, still standing, not the one that had fallen) and one hand shading her eyes to look down the road, and wisps of hair, not white then, not even gray, blowing across her face. She liked thinking about Mamaw that way. It was the way she used to imagine her when she was little.

Then they walked back along the road in the loose, hot sand, and he

pointed out the blackberry thickets along the fence row. She asked if
they could pick some, but he said it was much too late, blackberries
were in the spring. Mama had told her about picking blackberries, she
said, and how they ate almost as many as they took home. She pictured them there, innocent and berry stained. It was pretty to think of.

He nodded. He remembered berry picking, too, the warmth and the
thorns catching at them all over, the feared snakes forever gliding
under the brambles toward their bare feet. Where had it all gone?
Why had it gone? He remembered one hot spring day when the other
girls were picking unseen but heard, he and Edna Earle picking
together. He began to tease her about eating the berries she picked;
Mamma always said she ate as many as she carried home. Then, in
play, he fed her one: open, little bird, here comes a fat bite. And she
laughed and her beak gaped for more, her wet-warm mouth receiving
his fingers that worked in and out and in again, far into the wet
hollow, while she licked them, receiving the warm gush of berry juice
that soon smeared her face. They stood close in the embrace of the
heat and the thorny vines, the sweat running. Then Ora Lee popping
her head through, demanded what were they doing. Picking berries.
Too late now!

Too late, Lori thought. I was born too late for all that.

A truck plowing through the sand approached, passed with choking
cloud, and then stopped. When the dust cleared, they saw Randy and
Duane leaning out of Jess's pickup. Jerry was in the middle, looking
back at them through the glass. "Hey," Duane called, "we met Mama
and them on the road and told 'em we'd come and get you."

Elmo said he was going to drive her back, but they told him they'd
save him the trouble of hitching up. He hesitated. "Where's she goin'
to sit?"

"In my lap, I guess," Randy volunteered.

Elmo said no, she wasn't.

"All right, then, I'll ride in back. Will that suit you better, old
man?"

He still looked uneasy about it, but guessed he'd just as soon not get
out. So Randy jumped down and went around to the back end, and
Lori climbed in beside Jerry and waved goodbye. They dug out,
churning up great clouds of dust again, turned around abruptly in the
turn-in to Elmo's place, and roared back past him. When they rounded a bend, Duane stopped and Randy hopped out of the back and

came to the door again.

"You sit in Jerry's lap," he told her. "We're gonna give you a ride you won't forget."

They drove onto a blacktopped road, then took another rutted dirt road, veering off again at one narrower yet and still deeper in loose sand. They sloughed as they turned.

"Now hold on to ol' Jerry," they said.

Duane hit the accelerator sharply. The rear end fishtailed in the deep sand, while he swung the wheel, laughing. Then they gathered headway and plunged on, flying down the road to a deep crossroads, where he hit the brake and made them spin.

"Ooo-ee," the boys whooped. "Come on!"

She held on to Jerry and braced her foot against the floorboard, holding herself back from the windshield and the flying road. Again and again they tore down the road, one road or another, and stopped, careening and wallowing in the loose, deep sand. It was awful. She had never ridden like that before and she was scared silly, so scared that all she could do was laugh and squeal and clutch Jerry, while his oily hair whipped against her temples.

Jerry pulled her in against him while Duane slammed the truck through the sand harder and harder. When she felt his hand on her leg she jumped and said "Hey!" but he said he was only keeping her steady so she wouldn't hit the glass. After that she hardly noticed. All she cared about was lasting through this. The boys were silent now, looking at each other with expressionless faces while they careened along the roads from ditch to ditch, their bodies jolting together. At last, lethargically, they drove her home, where Jess and Ruth were playing another in the endless series of forty-two games with the neighbors.

IX

IT TURNED INTO A LONG WEEK. On Tuesday a letter came from Edna Earle with terse greetings for all and instruction for Lori: stay out of the sun at midday, show them how nice she was, have all her things together and ready when they came to get her on Saturday. That's so we can make a quick getaway, she thought, stifling the realization that boredom was beginning to make a quick getaway sound good to her, too.

On Thursday, another pink envelope came with a sheet of familiar flowered stationery. "Dear Sweetness," it began, "I hope you are having a nice time but wish you was home, can't help worrying . . ." She skipped over that part and picked it up again near the end. "Billie and Garth insists on coming to get you. I don't want them to, but Billie seems like she really wants to see Mamma and this is an excuse for her to go since we'll pay part on the gas. So I guess you'll be riding back with them, I'll be worried sick, you tell Garth to not drive to fast. He never had a lick of sense. I shouldnt do this but your father insists. If anything happens I'll never forgive him, but he says after all I didnt want to make the trip except to get you, which is true, and Billie does. How is poor old Mamma?"

It was a depressing letter. Couldn't she at least pretend to want to come see Mamaw? But at least Lori was glad to hear that Aunt Billie and Garth were coming for her, instead of her mother and daddy. That and her date for the movie were the two things she had to get her through the week.

Thursday was another long day. She tried to read in the hot front room, dim with a brown light filtering through the yellow window shades, but it was no good. All week she had tried to fill the time with reading, and still her bookmark set off only a quarter inch from the fatness of the waiting chapters. In the quiet, everything distracted her and annoyed her—a door slamming, a fly buzzing, Aunt Ruth gossiping in the kitchen with some visitor. She was irritable, and irritated with herself for having expected whatever it was that she had expected.

Lunch was cold butter beans and leftover fried steak festooned with white grease. Mamaw mashed her beans into a paste that she sucked from the tip of a spoon, making slow *schloop* sounds. The boys did not come in. Randy was stocking shelves at the grocery store for fifty cents an hour, and Duane simply stayed away, doing whatever boys do. Lori began to wonder if they remembered about the movie.

After lunch Aunt Ruth found some old yarn and a pair of knitting needles, and Mamaw tried, not for the first time, to teach Lori to knit. But her knobbed old hands cramped, and Lori's sweated. Mamaw went to lie down, and Ruth drove off to the washateria.

Lori went out back and surveyed afresh the black cow-piles clustered with flies and the drying garden with its weeds. Probably, she thought, she should go see if anything needed picking. But she didn't want to. She thought of going to sit under the bois d'arc tree in front, where the pale green horse-apples lay all around. She could sit there and write a letter to Elaine Tuttle, and maybe someone good-looking and clever would come along. But she couldn't think of anything to write to Elaine, and if Prince Charming had existed in Clamie she would have known it by now. So instead she retrieved her book and curled up in the porch swing, where the sluggish heat wrapped around her like a quilt tucked close by over-eager hands.

She must have dozed. Ruth was back, and Jess in from his milk run and some hauling he'd done. Mamaw coughed and sighed. Lori went to take a cool bath in the footed tub and plan what she would wear, or hoped she would wear, to the movie.

When the boys came in she waited, but they didn't say a word about it. At supper, still not a word. But finally, as if they'd been talking about it the whole time, Duane pushed back from the table and asked if she was about ready. Jerry would be there in a little while to get them.

Mamaw didn't want her to go. Movie houses were dark, and boys were likely to get fired up, cousins or no. Lori begged her to hush, they would hear her, but she didn't care. At least, she said, Lori could go change into something plainer than what she had on, her pink blouse and full skirt puffed into a bell by the big petticoat underneath. "You get all spruce and pretty and get them boys all fired up, you might wish you hadn't."

But Ruth assured her that everything would be fine. Jerry was a good boy, too. She changed the subject deftly: "Have you noticed how much Duane and Randy both are getting to look like Floyd when he was that age?" She got out an old picture of Floyd, and they started speculating where the boys and Lori got their height, their build, this feature or that. They couldn't figure out who she looked like. Some bit like the whole family, Mamaw said.

Jess, who had appeared to be asleep, piped up, "I bet she looks like you did, old lady." Ruth agreed. Lori had Mamma's height and maybe her nose. Mamaw said she didn't know; it was too long ago. But she looked pleased at the idea.

After Jerry picked them up, they cruised into town and rode up and down the three-block main street before heading in to the high curb. A few adults walked up, paid, and went in. But most of the audience were teens who lounged outside, tickets in hand, until the last minute before the show began. There were twenty-five or thirty of them. The girls nearest Lori said hi. They all wore full cotton skirts and sleeveless blouses, and they all eyed her full skirt and sleeveless blouse and made calculations about the petticoat underneath. The boys exchanged feints and drawn punches. Cigarette packs bulged in their pockets or rolled-up sleeves.

The picture was an old John Wayne film, *The Wake of the Red Witch*, which everyone present had seen at least once. The kids trooped up and down the aisle carrying popcorn and shooting wads of paper at each other. Here and there couples slumped into hard-breathing bliss. But everyone hissed and booed, as a matter of principle, when a gap and blurring occurred at reel changes.

After about fifteen minutes Jerry remarked that it sure was nice and cool in there. When she agreed, he slipped his arm over her shoulders and tugged her toward him, and they sat like that, immovably, for most of the film.

When there was half an hour or so until the hero would meet his watery doom, couples began drifting out. Jerry whispered near her ear, "You wanna leave?" but settled back when she answered, "No, why?" Then after a decent wait he whispered again, "C'mon, you know how it ends, doncha?" As if by prearrangement, Duane and Randy stood up, and they all filed up the sloping aisle.

Lori wondered why they had left before it was over. It wasn't a bad picture. They piled back into the car without a word and began to cruise those few blocks again: up and down, around the drugstore and behind the feed store, up and down. A couple of other cars doing the same honked each time they passed. At one end of the circuit, in a gravel waste marked off by a string of light bulbs, a knot of dateless males stood among the cars in front of Hyder's Cafe. On the third pass, Duane said, "Let us off here a minute, will ya?"

So then it was the two of them cruising alone, and this time when Jerry rounded the end of the feed store he kept going straight and they were headed past Aunt Ruth's and down the dark road. He kept his eyes on the path pushed open by the headlights, offering no explanation. They passed one dirt road narrowly interrupting the wire fences, then another, then turned at what was perhaps the third. Then they were careening along and spinning in the sloughs of crossroads as they had Sunday afternoon in the truck, but it was worse now because of the darkness. Jerry never said a word, only grinned and fought the steering wheel as they swerved and jolted. The only sound was the roar of the car. Turn after turn, roads all alike, until she was thoroughly lost. Then they stopped, and as the sand settled past the headlights she saw a tree trunk and beyond it an unpainted wall, before he switched the lights off.

He grinned at her proudly. "You like that? I knew we could show you a good time."

He sat with his head on the seat back and his arms spread as if to relax and catch a breeze. But there wasn't any breeze. It was all sticky night heat and the sounds of night creatures. She said her aunt would be getting worried about her, but he didn't think so. After all, they had left before it was over, and everybody always went around some after the show. Her aunt would know that.

Without warning he turned on her and pressed his nose against her neck, breathing down her collar. She felt goosebumps rise. Now what should she do? She hadn't counted on anything like this. He said she smelled good, moving his mouth against her as he talked so that she felt his chin against her collarbone. "I like it how girls smell," he said. Then he caught her under the chin and was kissing her mouth, hard, before she realized what was coming.

She pulled back to catch her breath and protest, but there he was again, chewing at her lower lip and pulling her blouse out from her skirt. This was not at all the way she had imagined it, and it was definitely more than she had bargained for.

"Hey now, quit it!" she protested. "Take me back!"

"Aw, you don't mean that." He caught hold of the arm that he hadn't already pinned against her and with his free hand fought up the billowing layers of pastel petticoat, shoved aside the crotch of her panties, and jammed his big middle finger into her.

Then she lost her nerve and went limp, beginning to whimper. Gratified, thinking that meant the end of her playing of the game, he moaned "Atta girl" and let go of her wrist. But when she heard the loud zip that followed, while his hands were occupied there, she lunged for the door. And in the sudden light when she opened it, there it was, as neither her imaginings nor her mother's warnings had quite shown it to her, red and huge in his hand with its one little eye staring her down.

X

SHE RAN. Then, seeing he didn't come after her, she crouched behind a bush until he drove off. When she couldn't hear the car any longer, she straightened up and looked around. It was very dark, and she remembered that she didn't know where she was.

Instinctively, for fear of snakes, she moved out into the road, thinking she might follow it until she reached the blacktop that would take her back into town. But which way? If she chose wrong, she would get more and more lost. She stood in the middle of the narrow, sandy road and looked up and down, trying to recognize something, trying to calculate how far they must have come. Toward her left it ran away straight between wire fences until it disappeared; not a cow, not anything broke the solitude that way. Toward her right it made a little dip, and dark blobs of trees drew near it. She was crying but holding back the sound with her hand so that whatever lay hidden in the vacant darkness would not hear and come after her.

Then she noticed a darkened old ruin, an abandoned house. She had seen its side wall in the headlights. Now, with her eyes adjusted to the half-moon light, she could see a fallen porch roof and weeds like small trees grown up through the floor near the front steps, or where front steps must once have been. Abandoned, it looked small and frail, like a skinny, gray old woman. It occurred to her that she recognized it. At least she hoped she did. There might be old deserted farm houses scattered all over this county, all looking alike. But this looked like Mamaw's old house, the house she had walked around with Uncle Elmo only last Sunday. It sat with its flank to the road just as she remembered. If she was right, just down that stretch of dirt road and past the dip, the low creek crossing where trees drew so close as to brush the sides of a car, there should be a turn to the left and then the rutted turn-in to Uncle Elmo's place.

She kept to the center of the road, where the pale sand seemed to give off a thin light of its own. It seeped into the toes of her sandals and out the backs. Darkness pressed in on her from the fence rows, and twice she heard a scuttering in the tangles of vines and weeds. She kept stopping to look up and down the road for car lights, but none appeared. That was good. Cars brought boys yelling things. They had done that at home, and she knew it would be no different here.

The dry creek crossing shut her in absolute darkness. They had said there were sometimes water moccasins here. She wondered what a moccasin looked like. Like the small snake barred with ruddy colors that her father had killed in the backyard once? One could be gliding toward her from the shallows right now and she wouldn't see it. Then she was running through the drained sand of the crossing where the sky was blacked out, up and out of that pitch darkness and along the short leftward stretch to where, sure enough, the narrow ruts marked a turn-in.

There was light in the window. The dog on the porch didn't bother to bark at this human he had smelled on his steps before, but only lifted his head for one look, sighed, and laid it down again. Then on the second knock her uncle was there, slow-moving and unwilling to look at her directly, his right hand working back as if it didn't know whether to slip into the pocket or not and the left sliding uneasily up and down the door. "What are you doin' here at this time of night?" he demanded.

She pushed past him and dropped into the single chair turned at an angle from the table. He must have been sitting there when she knocked. She saw his open Bible, lit by an oil lamp, and an open bottle. She put her head down on her arms and closed her eyes. Now if she could only count to three and when she opened them have it all be gone.

"How'd you get here, anyway?"

Still she pushed her face into the crook of her elbow and scrunched her eyelids tighter. She didn't want to talk to him. But he asked again, and she thought, yes, I'm going to have to tell him something. So she lifted her head and opened her eyes and looked at the dishes standing in neat and forlorn order on a shelf behind the table. There was a pathos in those three plates, those cups and bowls and two jelly glasses. They made her think, suddenly, that she could tell him all of it.

"We went to the show," she began. She told him about leaving Duane and Randy off at the cafe, and about Jerry's wild driving and his parking beside the road, and how she couldn't think of anything to talk about to him but it didn't matter because he didn't want to talk anyway.

But he didn't want to hear about it. He told her to hush, he already knew the rest. And when she went on anyway, about Jerry pulling at her clothes and the rest, he flailed his arms and yelled at her to stop, to shut up.

"He was awful," she protested. "I was scared of him and—"

He put his hands over his ears like a petulant child and stamped. His skin had gone gray as his hair, and he jerked his head and screamed "No!" like a child in a rage. After a minute he let his hands down cautiously, making sure she wasn't telling him any more. Then he pulled up the other chair and took a drink from the bottle on the table.

She was utterly vexed. Here she had come to him to take care of her, and he hadn't done a thing. Instead, he was making himself out to be the victim. He'd better get up from there and take her back to Aunt Ruth's right now, she told him. "That nasty Jerry! I hate him! Mama was right. Just like that John Pollard, I hate them both. I won't ever let another one close to me, never. Are you just going to sit there?"

He didn't pay the least attention to her, but just sat with one arm cocked over the chair back, watching the lamp flame and waiting for his slug to hit the right place, and then waiting for the next one to hit it better. Then he started talking. "Just the same all over," he mused. "Time and again the same. The sweet little girls and them boys gettin' after 'em. Just the same over and over."

He sat shaking his head and muttering for a while, then looked up at her. She had given up on him and subsided into sullen sniffling. "That's how it was with Ora Lee, of course," he said. "They kept gettin' after her till she didn't know what for." He shook his head and spat into the cold fireplace in disgust. "Ora Lee went off unmarried, and then Edna Earle and the rest went off to Fort Worth and I guess they was after her just the same. And then Billie, I heard about that, chasin' around with the boys and havin' all kinds of fun, till your mother set her straight. Always the same, boys and their nastiness, not just boys, grown men, too, and talkin' nastiness. Ruins everthing."

He had a far-off look, and she was almost afraid of him. He must actually be crazy. But she was detached, too, even from the outrage of her own encounter, now, detached enough to be curious about what he might say. This was the time, while she had him talking. "What was it with Jake Glover, really?" she asked. "Why did you do it?"

"Jake Glover," he mused. "Old Jake. He did have to turn up, him and his meanness and nastiness."

He took another slug and started telling her again how Jake Glover had shown up after all those years in the asylum and had taken out his revenge on the house, how they were scared all the time that fall, how Jake hung around Clamie watching Edna Earle when she went to school. "He was all mean-lookin' and squinty-eyed, scary-lookin' for sure. I'll tell you what he was: he was the devil. He tried to burn down this very house, right here where we're settin', just for meanness. Did you know that?"

It gave her the spooks. She could imagine spooky old Jake Glover slipping around out there in the dark right now with the kerosene can and the matches.

"And then they all went off, the whole family but me, just sold the place and moved off like it didn't matter. But even then things mighta been all right if I hadn't done what I done. Shot Jake Glover." He caught himself up. "But I told you that already, didn't I?"

"You never told me why. Really why."

"Nastiness, always nastiness," he began again. She didn't know if he was answering her question or talking about her misadventure with Jerry. "Just the same old nastiness, always the same. Mamma tried to keep us from it, to keep it away from us, so we wouldn't be thataway. I never woulda knowed nothin' about it if other boys hadn't talked. At school sometimes they talked that way about girls, sometimes about my own sisters, even, and we had to fight 'em, Floyd and me . . . well, anyway. It was after they had left and I was clerkin' at old man Badgett's store, and old Glover come in with that weasel look of his, grinnin' and talkin' nastiness. He leaned over the counter and kinda whispered so nobody but me couldn't hear him, and he said—" He jumped up and threw the half-full bottle into the fireplace. "He hadn't no right to talk that nastiness about her, not *her*, and askin' me if I hadn't thought nastiness about her, too, as if . . . He hadn't no right to. I done the Lord's work, I tell you! I tell you, I done the Lord's work if I did get Huntsville for it."

She was really scared of him, then, scared enough not to be curious at all about anything he hadn't told her yet. "You've got to take me back to Aunt Ruth's, you hear? Listen, you've got to take me back." She yelled it into his face.

Then he seemed to hear. Without another word he went out to

harness the old horse, with Lori along to keep her eye on him.

But just as she climbed up there was a honk and Duane and Randy pulled in driving Jerry's car. They remarked coolly, as if nothing had happened, that they had come to get Lori. So she was turned over to them once more, like a piece of baggage, and they turned around and headed back through the creek crossing and down the road without a word or even a direct look. At the first crossroad after they turned onto the blacktop, they stopped and picked up Jerry. They all three sat in front, leaving Lori alone in back, and drove in without saying a thing.

Back at the house Aunt Ruth and Mamaw were up and wringing their hands. But when Duane explained blandly that they had been out to Elmo's, where there wasn't any phone, and he had figured they would know Lori was all right because she was with them, Ruth was glad to accept that account of it without question. She woke Jess up, and they trailed off to the back bedroom. Late as it was, the boys went off again in the truck. Mamaw, who was already in her nightgown with a dress buttoned over it, stepped out of her slippers, took her teeth out, and climbed into bed, complaining of late hours and crazy young-uns. That was all there was to it for them, and Lori wasn't going to tell them any different.

She lay drawn up into herself on the far edge of the bed from Mamaw, and could not sleep. Mamaw snored and softly farted, and she lay there and hugged her disillusion. Nothing was right, nothing was any different here. Mamaw wasn't any different than she had been at home, only slovenly and cross and whining. Boys were no different. She herself was no different. What had been the use of coming here?

She slid out of bed and padded barefoot across the gritty floor of the bedroom and across the living room to the open front door. It was quiet outside, no sound except a backfire off in the distance. Boys cruising, she thought, looking for some girl to bother.

She stood there looking out into the dark, her gown clinging to her with dampness, and began to want to touch herself. It was like an urge to verify, to check and see that it was all still just as she remembered it. She lifted her gown and ran her hands and fingers over her breasts, her sides and pelvic bones, every inch. She felt herself roughly, punitively, so that the hair scrubbed against her skin. Then she slid an experimental middle finger into the opening groove. It was all the same. This night had made no difference; it had not really touched her.

She sat on the couch for a while with her knees drawn up under her chin and thought about the ugliness of what had happened to her. She was profoundly irritated that her mother had been proven right. That was the last thing she had wanted.

Then she knew what to do.

She slipped back through the bedroom and, from the corner, scooped up the clothes she had been wearing: skirt, blouse, pants, bra, petticoat. Then she went into the kitchen and found a pair of big black-handled scissors that she had seen there. She was very careful, very quiet, so as not to disturb the snoring that came softly from the back bedroom. Back in the front room, she sat cross-legged on the couch and took up her things one at a time. The blouse: she cut it up the back, hem to collar, across the shoulders, then into strips and the strips into little squares. Next the skirt: into two-inch strips, then two-inch squares, then smaller bits. It took a long time. There was a lot of cutting to do.

It was long after midnight and very quiet outside when she finished the petticoat. A big job, there was so much of it. And the more she cut, the madder she got—mad, now, more than humiliated. Mad at ol' Jerry, sure; madder at Duane and Randy, who must have plotted it with him. She made a vicious slash across one brassiere cup and worked that into little pieces. Then she cut through the elastic of her underpants.

She was waiting now for the boys to come in. She had dreaded it before, but now she was ready for them. She sat with the pile of strips and scraps on the floor in front of her, waiting.

It wasn't long. They came clomping in, sleepy and sullen-looking. Then they saw her and stopped, wary. Life was getting very complicated.

She had not decided until then what it was that she wanted with them, but now she made her demands, ticked them off on her fingers. They would slip into their room and get her a pair of jeans and a shirt. They would take the remnants of her clothes and get rid of them, however they had to do it. They would keep quiet about tonight.

They went off with a swagger but, having conferred, returned conciliatory, evasive-eyed. She was all right, wasn't she? So what was she thinking about doing?

Nothing, she said, not a thing. Only, if she ever did complain to her dad or to Jess or to anyone—and that's what she'd do if they ever opened their mouths about this—then just let them try to say they hadn't put him up to it. All she had in mind now was to get rid of those clothes and never see them again. As for being all right: "You better believe I'm all right, and I'm going to stay all right. No way a twerp like that is going to get anything on me, you hear?"

She stood glaring at them across the small dark space between the couch and the open front door. It echoed in her mind: "Someone'll get to you before you're fifteen." Well, she was fifteen and they still hadn't. She caught up the hem of her gown and in one pull stripped it over her head and threw it down. "See," she hissed. "Look all you want. It's all there and all just like it was." She could hardly believe it was herself standing there naked and unembarrassed before them, but she even prolonged the moment, exaggerated it, dragged it out to show them her invulnerability and how little they mattered. She positively spread her arms and flaunted every bare inch.

Then she picked up the patched jeans they had brought her and, with a forced deliberation, stepped into them, pulled them up, and snapped the grippers. Suddenly her bare breasts felt utterly vulnerable, after all, but still she made herself hold steady and face them until she slid her arms into the sleeves of their shirt and buttoned it up. "You can quit staring now," she told them. "Pick up that stuff and get out, leave me alone."

Then she had done enough, and she could let herself cry into the back of the couch. It was late, late, and she was so tired.

XI

LORI WOKE UP WITH A STIFF NECK and scum in her mouth, hearing a sound something between moaning and crying from the bedroom. She went to the door and found Mamaw sitting in the rocker, moaning and rocking back and forth, with her hands cupped together beside her cheek. "Poor little thing, poor little hurt thing," she cried. She rocked back and forth, lamenting. Her face was all streaked with tears that stood in the eroded hollows like rainwater in gullies. When she saw Lori she said again, "Poor little thing." She held out an unsteady hand closed around a pulsing bit of yellow fluff.

The canary. Its frightened black beads of eyes turned on Lori as she leaned close to look. One little forked twig of leg poked between the fingers. Only one. On the other side protruded only a tiny, blood-blackened stump.

"Oh Petey, Petey, poor little thing," she moaned. "A rat, a nasty rat, or a mouse must have got into his cage in the night and chewed it off, just ate it right off." She gathered the little puff to her cheek and sobbed. "And I slept right through it while he struggled and chirped for me. I ain't even fit to take care of a bird anymore."

Lori shuddered. Ate it off alive! It was sickening. She made herself take the bird from Mamaw's hand and carry it back to its perch. A tiny black drop formed against her finger. Then she helped Mamaw out to the kitchen for her coffee. What else was there to do?

Aunt Ruth stared at her unaccustomed clothes, but didn't mention them.

All day the bird sat huddled forlornly against the wire of the cage on its one leg, in fixed disregard of water cup or treat cup or cuttlebone. It would die, of course. All day Mamaw sat in the kitchen chair or her rocker, lamenting the mutilation and her own failure and her exile to a house where things could run loose in the night and eat life away. Her shakes got worse; she couldn't walk three steps without catching and holding to something. Toward afternoon she settled into a fixed resentment against everything and everyone, bursting out in accusations against the whole family and mixing up the names, Cleora or Floyd or Virgil, whatever came to her. There she sat in her rocker, with her clothes dribbled and redribbled and ever more pungent smelling, until five o'clock. Then she called for Ruth to help her to bed, and lay there drawn up with her eyes open and slack hands folded under her cheek.

At times during the day Lori felt her aunt looking at her with sly speculation. Had she guessed, then, or found the remains of the clothes? Or had the boys told? She didn't think so.

Billie and Garth arrived toward ten the next morning. Almost before the car had stopped in the swirling dust, Billie was out and shouting hellos. Edna Earle had once remarked that Billie dressed like a rainbow. She hadn't meant it as a compliment. And sure enough, she was bounding toward them wearing yellow shorts and a pink check blouse that any other redhead on earth would have known better than to wear. While Garth stood stretching and grinning beside the car, she dashed up the front steps and in with a bang of the screen door. Ruth and Jess looked at each other.

In a moment she was back and asking what was wrong.

Ruth turned up her hands and shrugged. "She's old, baby, that's all. She's just old."

Billie looked from one to another. "But she didn't even pay any attention to me. She didn't hardly notice I was there. That's not like Mamma. Why didn't you tell us she was like this?"

Ruth asserted stiffly that she was not to blame, she had done all a person could do for her.

Billie folded herself against the peeling porch wall, and Garth bounded up the steps and began to knead her shoulder. "She had to wear those shorts," he told them, as if it explained everything. "She did it to give the old girl something to fuss about. She laughed about it this morning, how her Mamma could always fuss." He stroked the top of her head and tidied her hair as one would a child's.

After a minute she shook herself and went in "to do for Mamma." For an hour she coaxed her through a sponge bath and a change of gowns and a little something to eat. Then she came back out on the porch, where, still in the boys' jeans and shirt, Lori leaned against a post. Billie sat down on the top step and wiped her face with her blouse tail. "How long has she been like this?" she asked.

"Since yesterday morning. The bird and all. I guess you saw that."

She nodded. "That's what Ruth said, that it was since yesterday morning." It was as if she had been verifying Ruth's account, trusting Lori's more than hers. She got up and leaned against the opposite post, fanning her midriff with her blouse, and eyed Lori. "All right, what's the matter with you, now?"

Lori shrugged and asked her what she meant. She knew she would end up telling her all about it, she even wanted to, but she wasn't ready yet. It would take some working up to.

"What do you think your mother is going to say about those clothes?"

"Ha! I know what."

"And you don't care? All right. But you know she'll ask questions."

Lori shrugged again. She had decided that she would never ever again put on girls' underthings and dresses. But it was a problem: that left her only the outfit she had on, no spare. She was trying to deal with the situation by pretending there was nothing the least bit odd about it.

She followed Billie around to the back, where they could hear Garth and Jess talking and laughing. Garth stood with his elbows on the top rail of the fence and one foot comfortably propped, ostensibly looking at the cow. Jess, beside him, was reared back, thumbs hooked in pants loops. As they approached, Garth leaned closer and talked faster, obviously finishing a joke, and then they both fell back and laughed and Jess clapped him on the back and called him Old Pro. "That was a good'n, Old Pro." Garth grinned. When Billie came up and tugged his shirttail for greeting, he turned his grin on her and gathered her in with an arm around her shoulders. "Feelin' better, hon?" he asked.

She nodded under his chin and said she guessed she was.

Rolling his quid to the other side, Jess spat and allowed that the old woman was failing right along now.

"Poor old Mamma." Garth patted her arm. "Hon," she said, "why don't you and Jess ride in and get gas now so we won't have to stop when we leave?"

Not a bad idea, Garth agreed, and they sauntered off, leaning their heads close to share another story. After a minute laughter drifted back, and then the starting of the car.

Billie hooked her arm through Lori's and asked if she was ready yet to tell her about it. They might not have another chance, she pointed out.

Lori was ready, and yet she wasn't. It was too hard to begin. The quiet shimmered around them like the heat, and they talked for a while about Mamaw and how sad it was to see her like that. There was a pause and Billie asked if she was glad to be going home. She guessed she was, or not so much glad of that as glad to get away from here.

"But it's not just because of Mamaw," Billie prompted. "Right?"

Lori looked at her, with the sweat standing frankly on her face and no makeup and her hair blazing in the sun. None of the others had that wonderful red hair, none except Cleora, who could never have been beautiful. Aunt Billie was beautiful, Lori thought, but in her own way, an easy and comfortable sort of way. Maybe it wouldn't be so hard to tell her, after all. She drew a big breath and started with Thursday night's movie, and then the driving. "And he parked the car and . . . you know."

Billie nodded. "But maybe you better tell me."

So she did, with a sick kind of feeling. But she went on anyway, through the hiding in the dark until he left and then finding Elmo's place, and then the boys coming and bringing her back. But not how Elmo had acted and what he had said, because he had trusted that to her and she would have to puzzle it out for herself.

She tried to hold her voice steady, but it wasn't easy. She didn't tell how she had confronted Duane and Randy later on in the front room, but only said that since Thursday night she had felt that they were laughing at her behind her back. "That filthy moron probably told them all about it," she fumed. "He probably even lied and made up more to tell than there really was. They do that, don't they? Boys are like, that, aren't they?"

Billie said that she guessed some of them were, but not all of them. But Lori was in no mood to reserve judgment. She ground her heel in the dust and gritted her teeth. "I hate him! I hate all of them! If they're not saying nasty things, they're grabbing at you. Mama's told me, they're all the same. I'll never get married, I know that. Then you have to let them grab at you anytime they want to, don't you?"

Billie caught Lori's arm and looked into her face with an urgency that surprised her, an urgency born of many years of dealing with Edna Earle and of finding her own experiences very different. "It's not always like that," she insisted. "It just depends. Don't pay any attention to your mother about that. Or, yes—" having worked herself into a corner she didn't like, "yes, pay attention to her, but . . ." Her look said that there were things she wanted to say but couldn't very well get into words. "You just got off to a bad start, you hear? Listen. There were times Garth could have talked about me like you say, but he didn't. And things haven't been a bit like you were saying, not for us. Understand? Just hold on a while. Wait and see." She threw her head back and blew a puff up over her sweaty upper lip.

But she had said enough. Not answers, no, but the possibility of freedom from her mother and from her own bad luck, if that was what it was. That was what Lori needed her to say. She might be her mother's daughter—and she was, in ways she could not know or ever be free of—but she didn't have to accept it; she could stand up against it.

Ruth called from the kitchen, where she was frying chicken, and Billie went up the back steps and in. A radio on the porch moaned "That's all she wrote, dear John, I brought your saddle home." Lori drifted around to the front. Maybe she ought to slip in and change after all. The jeans were hot, and they chafed between her legs.

In the front bedroom, Mamaw sat in her dimity gown by the window. Garth, perched on the sill outside, was razzing her: "Now, did you really do that? Come on, ain't no way a little bitty woman could do all that you say you done."

She pursed her mouth and beat a petulant cadence with trembly hand in time to her scolding. "Garth *New*comb, I *swan*, you are the hard*head*edest thing. I *told* you . . ."

He winked at Lori as she went by. "Oh, now, old lady," he teased, "now you are making' up a big one. You better watch that storytelling or I'm gonna sic the preacher on you."

"Now, Garth," she began again, but collapsed into weak chuckles while trying to keep up the pretense of scolding. She knew what he was doing. If she had been up to it, she would have given him measure for measure.

They understand how to deal with her, Lori thought. Garth and Billie do. I've watched and thought and still I don't understand anything.

After dinner, when the dishes stood in congealing grease around the table and Mamaw was back in bed and everyone whispering their last bit of talk, Lori tiptoed to the door to see if she was asleep, so she could say her goodbye. For a while she stood and watched her turn in the bed and fret. Then she went over and sat on the edge. "Mamaw," she said, "I'm going soon." She hesitated. What was there to say? So she lied. "It was good seeing you."

She lay with her back turned, and for a minute Lori thought she wasn't hearing, but then she reached back and caught Lori's arm with a grip surprisingly hard and drew her down closer. "You take care, you hear? You stay away from them boys."

Lori wanted to pull away, but she held herself steady. "Listen, Mamaw," she said. "You'll be back in Fort Worth by fall, I bet, and I'll buy you another canary."

"No, I won't," she whined. "They got me down her and they'll be glad to forget me. Tell 'em to come get me away from here, baby. You'll tell 'em, won't you?"

Was that all she was going to get from Mamaw? She needed more. Resisting the impulse to give up, she made one more try. "Would you rather have a parakeet?"

"No," she said, "they don't sing. Petey don't sing like he used to, either."

On inspiration she suggested that they might get him a girlfriend. He'd sing about that, wouldn't he?

"Oh, shoot, wouldn't he though?" She hid a toothless smile against the pillow. But then she sighed and shook her head. "No, Petey'll die."

"Then I'll get you a new one," she insisted. "A real bright yellow. And you'll take such good care of it, you'll make it the best singer yet. Okay?"

No response. It was no use. She disengaged her arm, stood up, and said again that they were about ready to go.

But Mamaw raised herself to her elbows and called her back. "Wait, baby. Listen," she urged. "Don't pay attention to all that. I don't mean to be complainy and take on so. Just don't pay no mind to that." She took Lori's hand and patted it, and told her what a fine girl she was and how much she loved her—wonderful, healing things. "I've always loved you the best of any of my own girls. You hear? Any of 'em, except Billie. She's my baby and the sweetest one."

Lori sat back down and laid her head on the pillow beside Mamaw's propped elbow. Now that it was too late, she felt like kicking herself for all her impatience and cross words. But Mamaw seemed to have forgotten it all, and to think everything was fine. With a twinkle, she said that sometimes she thought Lori was going to grow up to look like her. "Wouldn't your Mama have a fit if she thought that? A ugly old thing like me."

Holding hands, they laughed together at the thought. It was true; Mama would have a fit. She had different ideas for her.

"Now listen, honey," she said, "really, you take care of yourself, hear? And do your own way, don't pay no mind to old wore-out grannies like me. Nor don't pay too much to your mother, neither. I don't know," she made a little clucking sound and shook her head, "it seems like Edna Earle's turned out kinda hardlike. You just take care of yourself. Sometimes I wish you wasn't so schooly and booky, but that's just you, so you do your own way. And I know if you say you'll buy me another bird you will, and I'll be there to get it."

Then they caught each other up, and for that minute at least it was all all right, and Lori found herself feeling teary again but wouldn't allow it. She stood up to go. There were so many questions now, but time for only one. "You said you don't like being stuck off in the country. Did you not ever like it, even before?"

"Oh, well," she said, "it was different then. Or maybe I just didn't know any better. Anyway, it seemed different. Main thing is, then I could *do* and now I can't. That's the main thing. The rest don't matter."

Lori kissed her and said one more goodbye. Outside, Garth and Billie were waiting by the car, with Ruth and Jess standing by. They were exchanging last-minute bits of family news. Any word from Ora Lee lately? Floyd going in for tests, is he? Ruth turned her bland, conjectural gaze on Lori one last time and asked her to come spend a week with them again next summer.

She wouldn't for the world.

Then Lori got into the back seat and Garth put her suitcase beside her, and he and Billie got in front. They were backing out, waving, when the screen door opened and here came Mamaw, lurching out onto the porch and catching against a post. She waved frantically for them to wait. "Listen!" she called. "The next time I come to Fort Worth, I'll make you the biggest batch of tea cakes you ever had. You hear?" She waved again and turned back toward the door, and Ruth helped her in.

"Isn't she something?" Billie said. "Isn't she just the grandest thing?"

Lori felt choked. Mamaw wasn't ever going to make any more tea cakes, she knew that.

Then the house was too small to see any more, and in no time they were on the road to Paris, with Clamie dropping off behind.

Billie turned and looked at her over the seat back. "I'm glad you decided to change clothes," she said. "No use getting your Mama's back up. Have you decided what to tell her about the other things?"

No, she hadn't. And what on earth could she say? At the wheel, Garth whistled "Look down, look down that lonesome road," as cheerfully as if it were a jig, making a big show of not listening to what they were saying.

"That's what I figured," Billie said. "So I decided for you. Just tell her you forgot them, you left them here. I fixed it up with Ruth."

So they had been talking about her, then. She had been hoping they wouldn't but she guessed it couldn't be helped. Come to think of it, how had Aunt Billie known about the clothes? She had certainly not told her that part.

"Don't worry," she said. "I didn't tell her anything she didn't already know. I did tell her she ought to check up on those boys of hers a little more."

Garth, whistling one tune after another, never looked up from the road. He just kept driving. Lori wondered if Billie had told him about it, too, but decided that he, like Billie herself, was comfortable and safe. He was technically one of the enemy, but he didn't seem like it.

Billie sighed and shook out her hair. "We'll have to get Mamma back to Fort Worth," she said. "Ruth doesn't look after her right."

"The old girl's still somethin'," Garth commented. "She asked me how the Dodgers were doin'. Said Duane and Randy never would tell her even if she asked. Ain't that just the way of them two? But she's still a tough old bird."

Now was the time to make one last try at filling in the family picture. What had Mamaw been like back then? she asked. Back when they were all down here. "I used to imagine her like, oh, a hero, you know? Like in the history books, the pioneers and all. I guess that sounds silly."

Billie said it didn't sound silly at all.

"But then I'd look at her and she always seemed so helpless, in a way, or confused, like she couldn't understand things."

"Well, I guess she couldn't."

"A duck out of water," Garth said. "She's lived a long time, and things change."

Billie slid down in the seat and thought about it for a while. "Well, Mamma really was a kind of hero," she said, "in a way. With all she had to contend with. She had to do so much, and she did it. Not that she was perfect, I don't mean that. She had her warts, the same as now. She's cranky and backward. And set in her ways."

"Funny, though," Garth pointed out. "A real character."

"Oh, yes, she's that. But back then she was, I don't know, just Mamma. She took what came, and she did the best she could for us, in her own way. She was just herself, in her own time."

Looking out at the heat shimmers that beckoned and faded and at the road slipping past, Lori felt that it was a kind of key: she hung on, she did her best, she was herself.

"Sometimes I think you're a lot like her," Billie said. "Anyway, there's a resemblance. Anyone can see that." She yawned and stretched, then settled against Garth with her face in the hollow of his neck. "Oh, hon, am I tired!"

He chuckled low and lazy and ran his hand up and down her bare arm. After a while he began to whistle again, but softly, so she could doze.

Riding in back alone, Lori contemplated the back of Garth's head and the nice, companionable way he shared his shoulder for Aunt Billie's nap. Mama said that he would never amount to a thing, that he and Billie would never have a thing. It wasn't true. They had amounted to a lot.

The windows were down, and a nice breeze coming in. More of a wind, really. She stretched her legs and wiggled her toes in their dusty sandals. She was taking that dust back with her. That, and not much else. A few scars, maybe. Probably she already carried Mamaw's and Mama's scars before she came to add her own. There was no way to know. She could only let them all—the aunts, the uncles, the foremothers—all settle back into the old, frozen portrait. She yawned and rode west on Texas Highway 66, into her own reel of the moving picture.